Introducing Puppetry

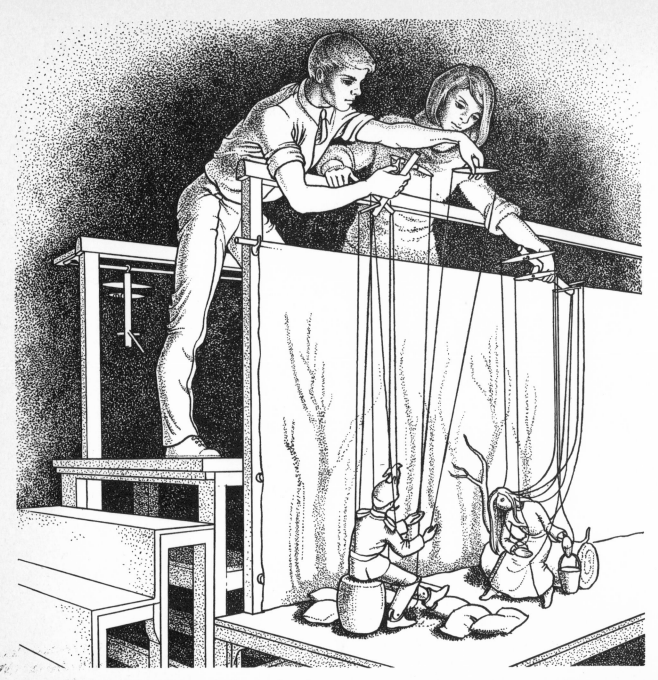

The position of manipulators at the leaning bar

Introducing Puppetry

Peter Fraser

B T Batsford Ltd   London
Watson-Guptill Publications   New York

© Peter Fraser 1968

First published 1968
Library of Congress Catalog Card Number 68–16175
68·106091 ?

Made and printed by offset in Great Britain by
William Clowes and Sons, Limited, London and Beccles
for the publishers

B T BATSFORD LIMITED
4 Fitzhardinge Street   London W 1   and
WATSON-GUPTILL PUBLICATIONS
165 West 46th Street   New York   N Y 10036

Contents

American readers please note the following equivalent terms or alternative materials

glove puppets = hand puppets
card = thin white cardboard
celluloid = acetate
craft knife = mat knife
fuse wire = any fairly pliable wire
sugar paper = construction paper
G-clamp = C-clamp
timber = lumber
macramé twine = nylon fish line

A Victorian children's theatre print

Introduction

Puppets can be classified in many ways: by the country of their origin; whether they are worked from above, below or from the side; or whether they are flat or solid. The puppets which have been most familiar in European countries in the past are glove puppets worked from below and marionettes worked from above. For this reason I have given more space to these two types than to others, but this does not mean that other puppets have less interest or scope according to their own nature. Also the techniques of construction described for glove puppets and marionettes can be widely applied.

When choosing the type of puppet with which you wish to work, you should first consider the nature and scope of each type of puppet, and the difficulties that may be met in construction and performance.

1 *The flat cut out figures* of the traditional Victorian Children's Theatre cannot, strictly speaking, be called puppets. I have included them because in a modern form they are a good introduction for very young children to the theatre itself, and to more advanced puppetry.

2 *Shadow puppets* are very quickly made, and many performers can be employed together if a wide screen is used, and in a performance involving spectacle and procession. The nature of the shadow puppet gives good opportunity for visual design.

3 *Rod puppets* may vary from a simple mechanism to a complicated one, but may be combined in the same production to suit the ability of individual performers. Rod puppets are particularly suitable for extra movements of head, eyes and mouth, combined with a spoken part.

4 *Glove puppets* provide a very close link between performer and puppet, and are more suitable for lively action and strong characterisation than for visual design. Any type of puppet may be used as a *persona* or mask through which the performer feels safe to reveal himself. Glove puppets are most readily used in psychiatric work involving projection techniques, particularly in connection with children.

5 *Marionettes* are the most difficult of all puppets to make and to manipulate, but they offer the extra scope of expression through complete body movement and all the opportunities for design in grouping, scenery and floor pattern.

I have aimed in this book to give as much information as possible in visual form, even in some cases drawing to the actual size of the finished puppet. Where the book is being used for instructional purposes I hope that students, with its help, may be able to cut joints, prepare plaster moulds, and do much of the construction and assembly of puppets without the need of constant supervision.

The sections on theatres, production, and sources of material may be of more help to instructors themselves. I have given with each type of puppet some guidance as to its nature and scope, so that a teacher may choose whatever variety is most suitable to his purpose, be it in visual design, woodwork, or drama and voice production.

Many people mistakenly see puppetry as an activity for children only or cannot appreciate it because they view it in terms of the live theatre. I see three aspects in puppetry. It may be seen as constructive play, and is so used in many schools today as part of an educational programme. Puppetry may be a commercial venture and has been increasingly used during the last few years in films and television. Finally it may be regarded as creative art. In other ages and in other cultures puppetry has been an important art form, and it deserves the same respect today.

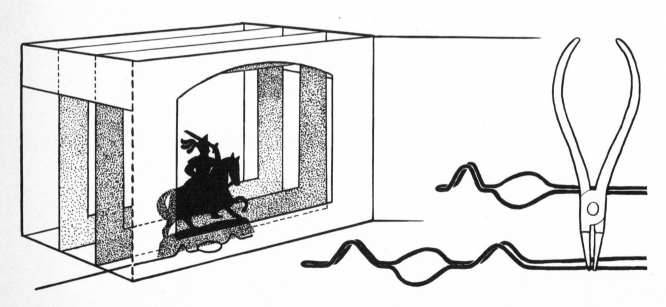

Cardboard theatre and wire bracket holders

The children's theatre

The traditional children's theatre belongs to Victorian days. In the nineteenth century prints of characters and scenery from the popular dramas of the time were sold 'penny plain and twopence coloured'. These prints were cut out, mounted on card, each actor being moved on and off the stage by means of a wire from the side of the toy theatre. The Victorian children's theatre has now become the property of the antique dealer, although reprints have occasionally been available. However, modern adaptation of the early children's theatre can give a great deal of amusement as a children's game and is also a good introduction to puppetry and the excitement and make-believe of the theatre as a whole.

The contemporary theatre no longer supplies prints of its scenery and actors, but nowadays there are countless coloured magazines available from which pictures of people, animals, cars, ships, aeroplanes and scenery can be cut and pasted on to card. A child's imagination can soon fit these into a story. For more advanced work characters and scenery can be traced and coloured from illustrated story books.

The theatre in its simplest form is made from a series of rectangular cardboard pierced screens, the front screen being the stage opening. The cut out screens behind form side wings leading to the back screen which is not pierced. A stage floor may be laid across the lower border of the rectangular openings in the screens, or alternatively the characters may be moved in from the side within the channels between the screens so that no mechanics of operation are visible. If you are using this second method the cut out figures must be mounted on card which raises the actor to the height of the stage opening, otherwise they will be seen only from the knees upwards. The easiest way to assemble the theatre is to cut out each part separately and then paste them together using long strips of thin paper to hinge the joints. Scenery for different performances can be hung from the top of each screen and held in place with paper clips. The general outline of each screen opening is followed, to allow a clear view of the backcloth against the rear screen.

Each actor, when cut and pasted on to card, may have a hinge of the same card turned back underneath, on which to stand. I prefer the wire brackets which give support from both sides of the flat card. These brackets are made of thin wire bent into shape by round-nosed pliers. The actors are easily fitted into these brackets when needed, and removed and packed flat between performances.

Shadow puppets

12

Shadow puppets

Shadow puppets belong to the Far East rather than to Europe but they have been seen intermittently in this country. In the late eighteenth century shadow shows known as *ombres chinoises* were very popular in London and Paris, and more recently there have been the shadow puppet films of Lotte Reineger who brings the art to a very high standard indeed.

Shadow puppets are shown in a darkened room, held from below, against a flat semi-transparent screen, with a light behind. The jointed flat figures are cut in outline to make a black moving silhouette. This silhouette can be pierced to add to pattern or detail, and colour can be added by covering pierced work with cellophane or celluloid tinted with thin oil paint. In scenery which is either pinned to a permanent screen, or painted or pasted on changeable screens, degrees of darkness from black to grey can be made by using various thicknesses of paper.

There are two main types of shadow puppet.

1 The Chinese style of shadow figure has a main control rod attached to the base of the neck at the front, and the weight of the body partly hangs from this point. The feet rest on a ledge at the foot of the screen and the screen itself is tilted forward at the top so that the puppets may rest in position without being held. Two further rods are attached to the hands, and a second ledge below the screen supports the rods when not in use.

The amount of jointing in the Chinese shadow puppet can be considerable as the figure will hang straight from the collar attachment. The movement is simple and limited by the use of the three control rods. Although hand movements are decisive, the general body movements are sinuous and flowing.

2 A second type of shadow puppet is supported on a stick held from below and pinned or glued to the lower part of the puppet's body. Limbs are moved by a system of leverage. Thin wire runs from the inner edge of each movable joint down beside the stick, and is then twisted round the stick to make a sliding sleeve. Looking at the picture of the trumpeter you can see that by sliding down the lower sleeve the arm is raised, and by sliding down the upper sleeve the leg moves outwards. The movements of this type of puppet are vigorous and decisive rather than subtle. They are shown against an upright screen

without a ledge and depend entirely on the support of the manipulator's hand to stay in position. However, a ledge can be placed below the screen and drilled with holes to house the rods of puppets which are to remain still for any length of time.

A combination of these two types of shadow puppet can be made where the figure is supported on a stick with some movements worked by leverage, and others by extra rods.

Design

In designing shadow puppets it is best to think from the beginning in terms of black and white, as this is how they will eventually appear to the audience. I never draw out designs in pencil, but start straight away with brush and indian ink and aim for a broad carrying effect before getting down to detail.

Shadow figures are most successfully designed from side view, though it is worth trying a front view figure now and again. Greek vase paintings and Egyptian wall paintings deal very well with problems of silhouette design and arrive at a side view of legs and head and arms, and a three-quarter view of the body. The Javanese shadow figures in the Victoria and Albert Museum are well worth looking at too. Costume can be used to fill out silhouettes in interesting and varied ways. The amount of movement in any figure depends on the demands of the character, but the fewer the joints the greater the stability. The height of shadow figures is entirely a matter of choice. Some of the eighteenth century *ombres chinoises* were only 6 in. high, but Javanese shadow puppets are at least three times this size. Because of the limitation of movement in shadow puppets it may be necessary to design two or three varied positions of one character for different scenes in a play.

Construction

The parts of the figure are traced from your original black and white design on to stiff card which should be black if possible, or painted black. The card may vary in thickness with the height of the puppet, but should remain erect when the puppet is held upright from below.

A   Cut out the broad outline of the figure first with a pair of scissors. Details and pierced work are best cut out later with a craft knife or razor blade, the card lying flat on a wooden board.

B   Joints are designed on the principle of overlapping circles with a centre shaft. The simplest method of attaching joints is to thread them with fishing twine close knotted at either side. Knots should be painted with thin glue for safety.

C   For Chinese shadow figures, I find that fencing wire makes a suitable rod. The end to be attached to the figure is bent into a loop with round-nosed pliers.

D   A second loop of fine fuse wire can be passed through the loop on the rod and fixed to the puppet, by being glued under a small cardboard section.

E   The free end of each rod should broaden to a handle grip. Adhesive tape bound round the ends soon builds up the substance needed, and can be covered with a whipping of fine cord. There is no rule for the length of the rods, but they usually project below the screen by the length of the figure itself.

With the second type of puppet I use fuse wire which is quite strong enough for the weight of leverage in cardboard limbs, and can hardly be seen where it stands free of the outline of the figure.

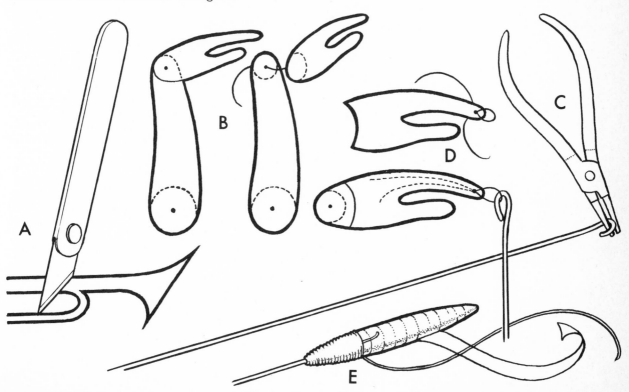

A screen for shadow puppets

The screen for shadow puppets is made from a simple wooden frame on which thin translucent material is tightly stretched. This frame may be fitted into the proscenium opening of any theatre designed for puppets worked from below and for shadow productions the width is more important than the height.

With the Chinese style of shadow puppet, the shadow screen is tilted slightly forward at the top and has a ledge covered with some non-slip material for the puppets to rest on near the base of the performer's side of the screen. The puppet is thus supported in position against the screen and the operator need only move the limbs. A further ledge below the screen can support rods which are not being used. For shadow puppets supported on rods from below the shadow screen need not be tilted.

Scenery for shadow plays may be pinned to the cloth of the screen between acts, or, while the curtain is closed, the whole screen may be removed and another put in its place with the scenery already pinned or painted on. Scenery is quite successfully made from cut paper or card. Various thicknesses of white semi-transparent paper can give a variety of shades from black to grey. Although the shadow figures are placed behind the scenery, they will not appear so to the audience.

A single light source should be sufficient in a darkened room to light the screen from behind. The light should be high enough above the screen not to cast on it the shadow of the operator, and just far enough away from the screen to light the whole of it.

Rod puppets

Rod puppets, like glove and shadow puppets, are worked from below. The manipulator holds the main supporting rod to the body in one hand, and with the other moves the rod attachments to the arms, and in some cases to the legs. The puppets themselves range from a simple development of the glove puppet, to a fully jointed figure comparable to the marionette.

This type of puppet has seldom been seen in Europe, and at its best belongs to the Far East. The Javanese rod puppets in the Victoria and Albert Museum are of as high a standard as the shadow puppets from the same country.

More recently, rod puppets have been widely and successfully used in America, with experiment in added range of movement and interest. The lack of any strong tradition in the rod puppet is perhaps a good reason for a free approach, and of all puppets I think they are the most suited to the demand many audiences now make for eye and lip movements related to speech. Details of these mechanisms are given in the section on special effects. Most of such movements are worked by a trigger mechanism which fits very easily to the main support of the rod puppet. In glove puppets the important index finger and thumb are otherwise occupied in arm movements, and in marionettes, where the whole body movement is of primary importance, the stringing is already complicated enough.

The illustrations in this section show a variety of types of rod puppet, from the most simple glove and rod puppets to the complete jointed figure. Rod puppets may be made of cloth, *papier maché* or wood. I give no details of these types of construction here as they are fully dealt with in the sections on glove puppets and marionettes. However, because of the ease with which rod puppets can be clothed, and because of the good control of arm movements by rods, I do favour a cloth body and limbs, with *papier maché* head, hands and feet.

As with other types of puppets worked from below, rod puppets present a problem when the manipulator's arm tires before the action is over. A projecting ledge fixed below the proscenium opening can be drilled to house the main supporting rods of the puppets. This mechanism is similar to that used with shadow puppets, but it goes further in that rod puppets can be rotated from side to side in their housings and still continue to make individual limb and head movements.

In America, Marjorie Batchelder has made movable stools on wheels which carry both the operator and the housing mechanism for rod puppets.

Construction

1   This is a combination of the rod and glove puppet. The head and hands may be of *papier maché* or wood and the rods of strong wire or umbrella ribs. Umbrella ribs have a hole already pierced in one end and are usually black so that apart from trimming to length they are ready for use straight away. A loop of strong twine or thin wire passes from the rod to the attachment on the hand. With a wooden hand the attachment is a screw eye in the palm. With a *papier maché* hand a wire loop in the palm must be part of the original framework.

The glove body is best made from blanket material which gives an appearance of substance over the shape of the operator's hand. The arms are made of stuffed stocking material sewn close at each end, and tied tightly at the elbow joint like a division in a string of sausages. Such a body is quite convincing when dressed in loose clothing which can easily be removed for pressing and cleaning.

The movements of this puppet have more range than those of a simple glove puppet, though both of the operator's hands must be used, one in the glove with the index finger in the neck, and the other to control the hand rods. When either hand of the puppet is not in use the rod may be allowed to hang loose.

2   A short wooden dowel rod passes from inside the glove to the head of this puppet. The shoulder piece, to which the arms and glove covering are attached, is a narrow oval of wood or *papier maché* drilled in the centre to allow for the passage of the rod. The shoulder piece rests on the index finger of the hand in the glove, and the head has the advantage over the previous puppet in being able to turn from side to side. The control of the rods to the hands prevents the whole body from turning when this movement is made.

3   The third puppet has the addition of legs free swinging from the waist. The legs like the arms can be made from stuffed stocking material but sewn across for a hinge movement at thigh, knee and ankle.

The glove for this puppet is made of dark material to be as inconspicuous as possible behind the legs. The upper part is clothed in the normal way, and the legs only in the lower part. Although there is no controlled movement of the legs, they may be swung over the proscenium ledge if the puppet is in sitting position. This movement can be quite convincing in both glove and rod puppets.

These three puppets are limited in size by the extent of the operator's arm and hands. The length of the rods is measured with the length of the manipulator's arm. When the puppet's hands are fully extended above its head, the rods should still reach beyond the operator's elbow, or the ends will show above the proscenium ledge. Clothing with any of these puppets may be drawn in at the waist to give more shape to the body.

Rod·and glove puppets

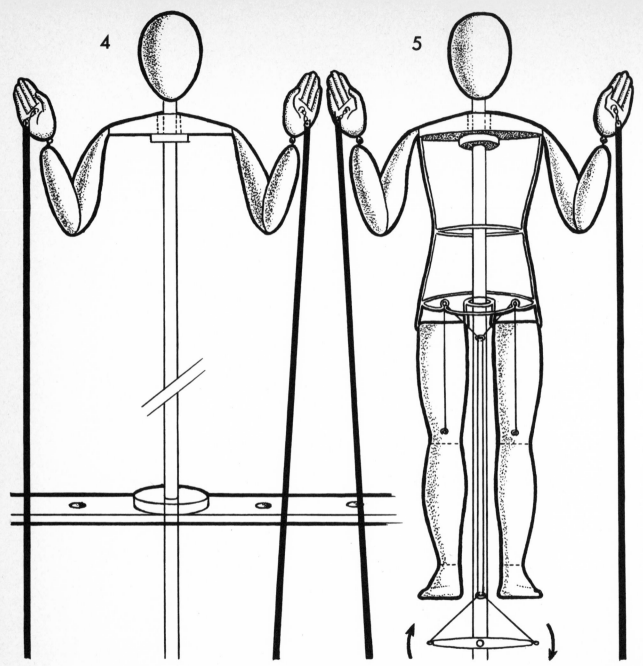

Rod puppets

4   This is a simple design for any long clothed rod puppet of any size and is capable of much adaptation. Since the operator's hand is now held at the bottom of the rod, the shoulder piece must be supported on a disc, either of wood or metal, firmly attached to the base of the neck length. In the diagram shown the only movements performed are arm movements and head rotation. However, any extra movements within the head itself, mouth and eye movements for example, are most easily added to this type of rod puppet. The strings from the mechanisms within the head pass through holes drilled on the neck disc, and down the main control rod to a trigger mechanism convenient to the operator's hand. At the base of the main control rod a suggested supporting ledge for puppets at rest is shown.

5   In this rod puppet a hollow wire framework body hangs from the shoulder piece. The framework may be made in many ways, but here it has an oval section at the waist and another at the hip joint. In the front of the lower oval are two loops in the wire to allow passage for the leg stringing, and also, at this level of the body framework, the centre wooden rod support should be loosely confined within a wire ring.

Stringing from above the knee joint passes up to the projecting edge of the body, and from thence to a screw eye in the centre rod. This screw eye is shared by the stringing to both legs which now pass down the centre rod, through another common screw eye and outwards to each end of a swivel control bar for alternate leg raising movement.

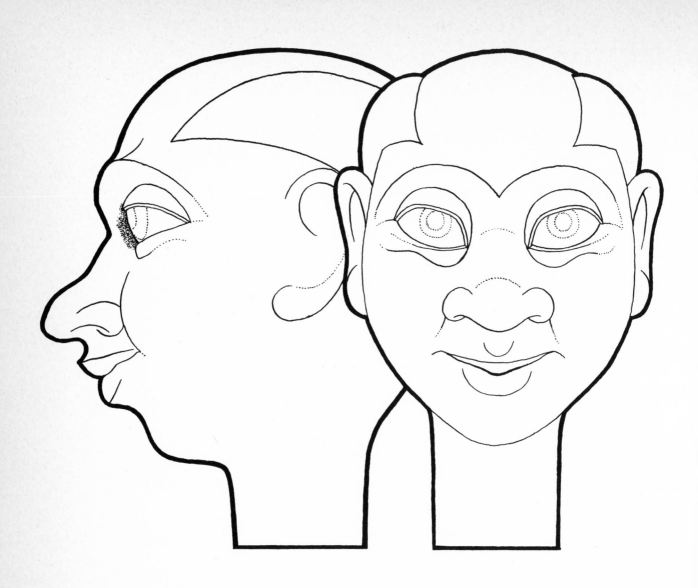

Drawing for the head of a glove puppet
'Quince' from *A Midsummer Night's Dream*

Glove puppets

Glove puppets are worked from below and follow the movement of the hand and fingers of the operator. Usually the index finger fits into the head of the puppet and the thumb and middle finger fit inside its arms. This method of operation is not symmetrical in appearance, but the thumb and index finger are most useful in gripping and holding movements. No other disposition of the fingers does this so effectively. Apart from gripping, holding and head nodding, the individual movements of glove puppets are very limited, although the whole puppet can move about within the performance area as quickly as the operator can move his arm, as they are so closely linked. This directness of control makes the glove puppet particularly suitable for strong characterisation for, in spite of its limited power of physical expression, there is no mechanical barrier between operator and puppet. Glove puppets are therefore very suitable for beginners.

Glove puppets may be made of *papier maché* or wood. I cannot feel that a head made from cloth is successful as there is little opportunity for modelling or expression, and this is important in glove puppets where the head and hands are the only means of creating character. *Papier maché* is used in two ways—laminated *papier maché* and *papier maché* pulp. These may be used separately or in conjunction and can be modelled direct over a core or used to fill a mould.

Laminated papier maché

For this type of *papier maché* an absorbent paper is necessary and although newspaper is often regarded as the basis of all *papier maché*, sugar paper, or paper towelling are much better for fine work. Sugar paper can be bought in different colours so that the building up of layers can be evenly done with one colour at a time. The paper is torn into pieces convenient for soaking in glue size, keeping them in their separate colours. Size is bought in crystals and is used in a ratio of a quarter of a pound to half a gallon of water. The crystals are soaked in the water for fifteen minutes then heated until the crystals melt. The torn up paper is placed piece by piece in the melted size until thoroughly soaked, then squeezed out gently and removed ready for work. Laminated *papier maché* is built up of four or five layers of paper so prepared, each layer being pasted to the next with flour or thick cold water paste. This may be done as direct modelling over a plasticine base or by filling a mould thinly greased. The first layer is laid directly in contact with the mould or core without paste, and thereafter paste is used on both sides of each layer. Paper pieces are torn smaller to fit the shapes required, and when the layers are completed the surface is pressed and rubbed smooth with a finger wetted with paste. The speed of drying can be increased by placing the work in warm air over a radiator or in the oven. The *papier maché* should be prised loose with a knife, then removed from its core or mould before it is completely dry, as it can still be bent slightly to pass over undercuts.

Papier maché pulp

For *papier maché* pulp newspaper is traditionally used, although I prefer paper towelling which makes a cleaner light coloured pulp. The paper is torn into very small pieces, a quarter of an inch square if you have the patience, scattered and mixed into a bowl of water and left to soak over night. The amount of paper needed for the head and hands of one puppet is about four double pages of newspaper, or a corresponding amount of paper towelling. When the paper has been soaked, it is thoroughly sifted and rubbed between the fingers while still in the bowl, then removed, squeezed out and pounded and kneaded on a slab until it is of as fine a consistency as you can possibly make it. This pulp forms the fibrous part of your *papier maché*, and to this is added modelling clay and ceiling whiting powder, each of about a quarter bulk of the paper pulp. Lastly glue is added, about a quarter of a pint of thick melted size. Some people use flour paste here but it takes longer to dry and has a very unpleasant smell in drying. Glue is mixed in, little by little, until the pulp can be rolled into pellets which do not crumble. This type of *papier maché* can be used for direct modelling over a core, or to fill a plaster mould. When it is dry the surface can be smoothed with sand-paper and sealed with a coat of thin varnish ready for painting.

Modelling a head in plasticine

For both direct modelling with *papier maché* over a plasticine base, and for making a plaster cast, a plasticine head must be modelled on a wooden peg stand. The following diagrams may help to show how a head can be built up in simple stages. Before beginning your model it is a good idea to make a drawing of the characters you wish to create. If the drawing shows both front and side views, you can turn the plasticine model on its stand to make frequent compari-

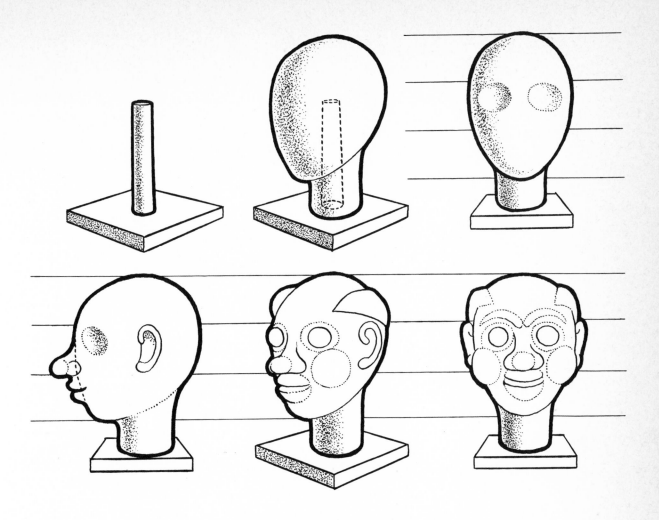

sons. The profile comparison is particularly important for beginners who often tend to make the face too flat. It may be helpful at this stage to have a look at the diagram on the proportions of the head in the section on marionettes. The early stages of the modelling may be done with fingers only, and the finer details with a wooden modelling tool. The head and hands of a *papier maché* glove puppet can be made either by

1 direct modelling or
2 lining a plaster cast made from a plasticine model.

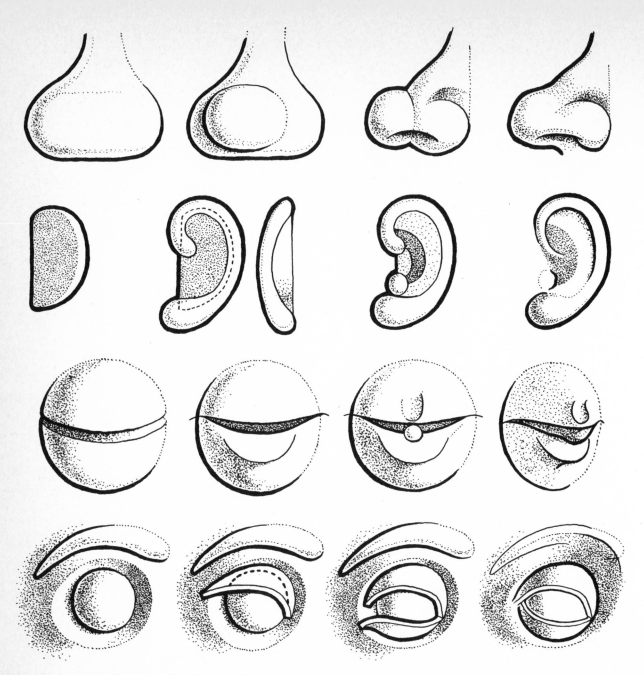

Building up the features of a plasticine head

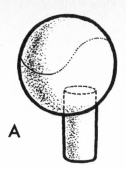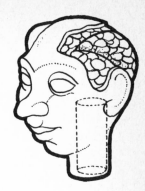

Direct modelling in papier maché

A Direct modelling over a permanent core

For direct modelling with *papier maché* a tennis ball pierced by a cardboard tube makes a good permanent base on which to build the head and neck. The cardboard tubing should be rolled round the index finger to make sure of an easy fit, and glued into a round hole cut in the tennis ball. The ball and tube are then bound round with a narrow bandage or torn rag to provide an absorbent base for the *papier maché*.

Laminated *papier maché* is used first to build up a simple basic shape with a suggestion of a nose, chin, forehead and ears. Plenty of paste should be used between the bandaging and between the layers. When the laminated coat is partly dry, the finer modelling is added, using *papier maché* pulp. A coat of paste or glue over the laminated coat helps to keep the pulp in place.

Modelling with pulp is different from modelling in clay, and shapes are formed by pressing and pinching rather than by building up. When the pulp layer is half dry it is best to repeat the modelling pressure over the whole head to compress and spread the pulp. This guards against possible cracking caused by shrinkage in drying.

B Direct modelling over a plasticine base

A second method of direct modelling may be used over a plasticine base from which the dried *papier maché* head is later cut and re-assembled. For this method the plasticine base must be fairly simple, as detail is lost in the added thickness of the *papier maché* coating. Laminated *papier maché* may be used on its own here, and the paper must be thin. Torn up pieces of paper handkerchief follow the plasticine contour very well.

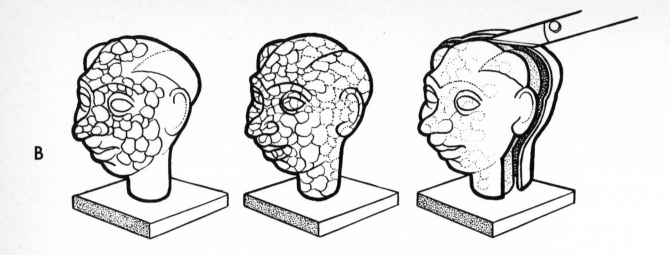

B

The first layer of paper is laid in small pieces directly in contact with the plasticine model without paste. A further four or five layers are pasted on and the last smoothed into shape with the finger. A wooden spatula or modelling tool helps to define the finer edges of eyes, nose, mouth and ears. When the *papier maché* is nearly dry it is cut with a very sharp blade into two halves—the face and the back of the head and neck from behind the ears. The rear half of the head may be prised off with a knife. With the front half of the head it is safer to remove the plasticine carefully piece by piece from the *papier maché* shell. Finally the two *papier maché* halves are pasted together from the inside with paper hinges, working through the hole in the base of the neck, and the whole of the inside lined with strips of bandaging for extra strength.

C

Making a plaster mould

There are two ways of making a plaster mould.
A by pouring liquid plaster into a box frame surrounding the shape to be moulded.
B by applying the plaster as it thickens directly on to the inside shape.

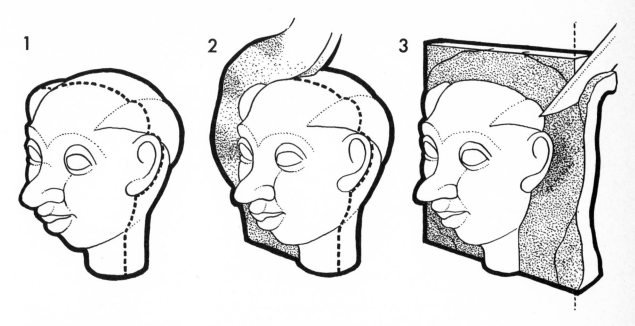

A Box method

1 The plasticine head is placed on a sheet of thin paper on a flat board. A faintly incised line is marked across the top of the head from ear to ear, and from below the ear to the base of the neck on each side. This divides the head into two sections for a two-piece mould.
2 A flat ribbon of clay or plasticine is rolled out and trimmed to a neat edge. This ribbon is placed against the incised marking on the head and firmly pressed into position up one side of the neck, round the rim of the ear, over the top of the head and down the other side.
3 Using a sharp edged tool the plasticine ribbon is built out at the corners and trimmed into a square.

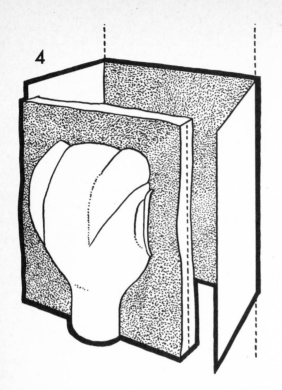
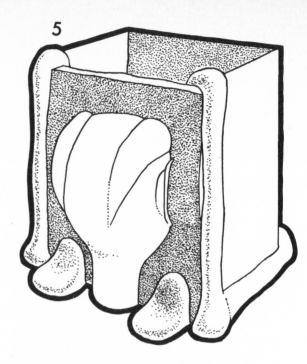

4 A folded piece of strong cardboard encloses the front half of the plasticine head.

5 The joints of the cardboard enclosure are sealed all round by rolled out lengths of plasticine and pellets of plasticine are pressed against its walls for support. The first enclosure is now ready to be filled.

6 Pour sufficient water into a two pint jug to fill the cardboard enclosure. This measurement can only be done by eye but when in doubt it is better to have too much than too little. Plaster of Paris is rapidly shaken into the water until the powder remains showing above the water level. The powder and water are now sifted together by hand until the liquid begins to show signs of thickening. It should at this stage be of the consistency of cream. Holding a corner of the supporting board in one hand, pour the liquid plaster of paris in a steady continuous flow, until the enclosure is filled to the top. The board should be shaken slightly during pouring to free any air bubbles from under the chin and nose of the plasticine model. Within a few minutes the plaster begins to set becoming quite warm in the process.

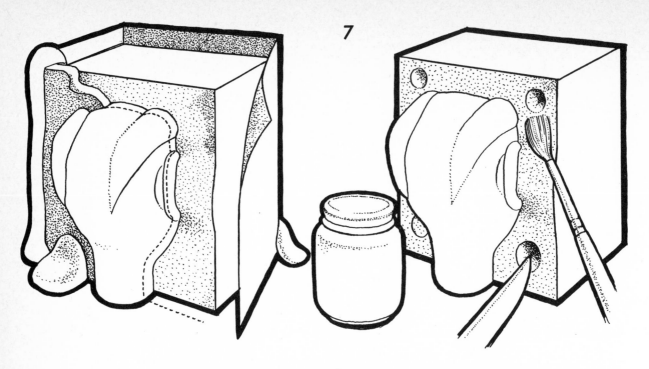

7 After about a quarter of an hour the first half of the plaster mould should be firm enough for the removal of the cardboard enclosure and plasticine division. Four holes are scooped out at the corners of the inner surface of the mould. These holes ensure an exact fit with the second half of the mould which can now be made. This inner surface is painted with vaseline to make sure that the two halves of the completed mould can be taken apart easily.

8 A cardboard enclosure is fitted to the first half of the mould and sealed as before with rolls of plasticine and pellets for support. Extra support may be given by tying a cord round the enclosure and the completed half of the mould. The enclosure is filled with liquid plaster of paris in the method already described.

9 When the second half of the mould has hardened, the cord, cardboard and plasticine supports are removed. By inserting the point of a wooden modelling tool at the joining of the two halves of the mould the second half is prised away from the back of the head. The original plasticine model is removed carefully piece by piece from the front half, and all the inside surfaces are cleaned with a paint brush and soap and water. The two halves of the mould, when thoroughly dried in a warm place, are ready to be filled.

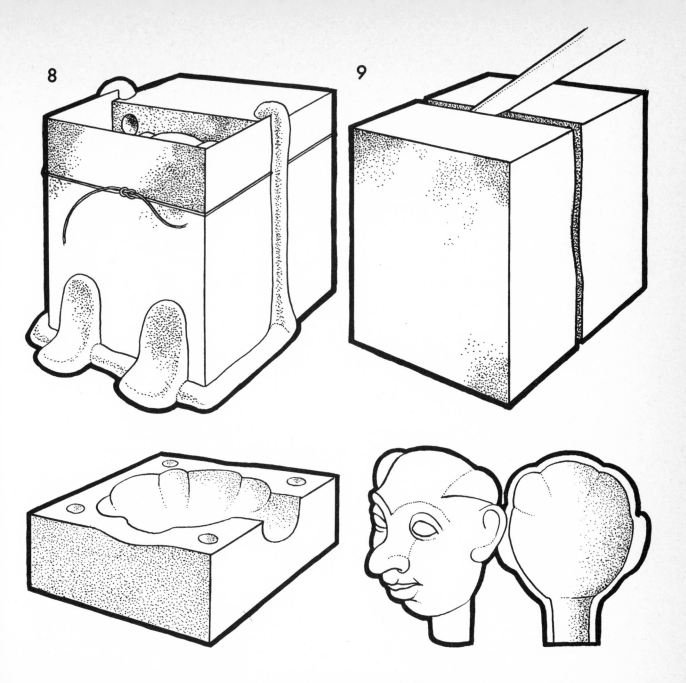

8

9

Completed plaster mould with *papier maché* linings from each half

33

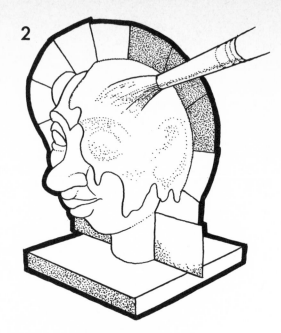

B Direct application of wet plaster of paris

In this method of making a mould the plasticine model is left on its stand.

1 A faintly incised line is traced over the top of the head, round the rim of each ear, and down each side of the neck. Thin plastic or metal sheeting is cut into small wedge shapes which are pushed edge to edge into the incised line, dividing the plasticine head into two sections. All the upper surface of the wooden stand is painted with vaseline, and also the surface of the dividing wall.

2 When the plaster of paris has been mixed, a first coat is run on to one side of the plasticine head with a large water colour brush. This thin coat is worked into all corners of the modelling, and successive coats build up the thickness as the plaster begins to set. The final layers may be scooped into place by hand and smoothed into shape making an inch thick shell of plaster of paris over the plasticine model. Strips of bandage can be pressed on to the surface of the plaster to strengthen the mould.

3 The same process is repeated on the opposite side of the plasticine model. When the plaster has set hard the two halves are prised apart, the plasticine core is peeled away, and the inside surfaces are cleaned with soap and water.

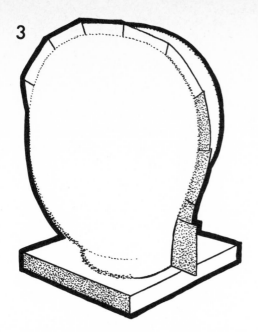

4 This drawing shows an extra division in the preparation for a three-piece mould. When there are deep undercuts in the modelling this is necessary to enable the eventual lining to be lifted out.

The direct application method of making a plaster mould is very much quicker than the box method, but some previous experience with plaster of paris is necessary before attempting it. The liquid plaster must be applied just at the right moment of setting, or else it will run all over the floor, or set hard on the brush before the work is complete.

Lining a mould

Each half of the two-piece mould is lined in turn with any of the following materials—laminated *papier maché*, *papier maché* pulp, plastic wood, or any other modelling substance that will set hard.

Laminated papier maché is built up from several layers of fine absorbent paper in each half of a mould painted on the inside surface with a thin coat of vaseline. Sugar paper is too thick for this purpose and I find that small pieces of torn paper handkerchief follow the shape most accurately. When the laminated *papier maché* lining is nearly dry it is prised out carefully with a knife. The two halves are then joined together on the inside with strips of bandaging, and the outside seam can be concealed by an extra layer of paper.

Papier maché pulp is placed in the greased mould in pellets, and firm pressure on the pellets welds the coat into one. The pulp lining should overlap the edges of the mould slightly to allow for shrinkage. When the pulp lining in each half of the mould is partly dry, the whole coating should again be squeezed firmly with the thumbs to counteract shrinkage and to re-define the shape underneath. The overlapping rim of the pulp layer is now trimmed, the edges painted with glue, and the two halves of the mould are pressed firmly together with the interlocking pieces in place and tied round with a piece of string. The mould is left in a warm place to dry out thoroughly, and when the two parts of the mould are divided, the head remains complete. The glued joint is trimmed and smoothed with sandpaper.

Plastic wood is either bought in tins or made from glue mixed with sawdust. Two pancake shapes are spread out first on a board and then fed into each half of the plaster mould like pastry into a dish. This must be carefully done so that the plastic wood layer is not broken. When each layer is in place, the surface is pressed all over to make sure that the mould and the lining are in contact. The edges of the lining are trimmed, painted with glue and joined together while still in the mould as in the *papier maché* pulp method. With plastic wood there is no need to use vaseline on the inside surface of the mould. Instead the whole plaster mould must be soaked in water before applying the plastic wood lining, and sometimes afterwards to help prise the two pieces apart.

The heads made from a plaster cast are hollow and therefore can be fitted as they are on to the index finger of the manipulator. If the hole in the neck is too wide an extra lining of *papier maché* can reduce it to the proper size, or a cardboard tube to fit the finger can be added.

Direct modelling of hands

Hands can be directly modelled in *papier maché* pulp over a permanent wire framework. This framework is extended to be coiled round a short piece of cardboard tube into which the operator's thumb or third finger will fit. The wire hand must be bound with bandage or strips of rag to form an absorbent surface for the *papier maché* pulp, and a coating of glue or paste over the bandaging helps to keep the pulp in place. Just before the pulp coating is added the fingers of the framework can be adjusted to any position you wish.

Carving a head and hands in wood

Choice of wood

The fine carving of head and hands demands a close-grained hard wood. All fruit woods, pear, apple, box and lime have this quality, but limewood is by far the most easily cut, and has a slightly waxy quality which does not readily splinter. The soft wood of the conifer tree is only suitable for the limbs of a puppet. If you buy your wood from a timber yard it should be well seasoned and ready to work.

Balsa wood is disappointing to use, as any cutting instrument other than a razor blade tends to crush the wood as the incision is being made.

Tools

A full set of specially designed wood carver's tools is very difficult to find nowadays. Without skilled training they cannot be used effectively, and for most purposes of carving a 1-in. firmer chisel for broad work and a $\frac{3}{8}$-in. chisel for fine work will do very well provided that they are kept well sharpened. Other tools that you will need are a mallet, a file and a small needle file and sand-paper if a smooth finish is needed; also a saw or plane to shape the wood into a rectangle ready for carving.

One important feature in wood carving is the need to keep the wood in a fixed position while it is being carved. In the early stages a table vice and 'G' cramp can be used. For finishing work a carver's screw is useful if you can get one, but I usually work towards the end holding the wood in a cloth in one hand, while the other hand is working at hand paring or filing. As work progresses it becomes difficult to hold the work in position without damaging the carving. I always leave the ears until last so that the head can be held in place from each side in the vice. Pressure from the top of the head to the bottom of the neck does no damage either. A carver's screw can fit into the underneath surface of the neck.

The carver's screw is part of the equipment of the professional wood carver. It holds the work from below by means of a screw shaft and is held itself in a socket in the work bench. A useful substitute can be made by screwing a block of wood on to the base of the head being carved as a temporary fixture, and holding the block in the vice.

Wood grain

An understanding of the grain direction of wood is essential if you are going to carve successfully. In the standing figure of a puppet the grain direction is vertical from top to bottom except in the feet of a marionette. Chisel cuts must always be made at an angle moving in the same direction as the grain. If this principle is forgotten essential parts of your carving will split off.

Carving the head

Unless you are an experienced wood carver, it is always safest first to make a drawing of front and side profiles and also a plasticine model of the whole head. When you begin to cut your wood you will then know exactly the shape you are aiming for and give more attention to the work of cutting.

1 Your wood may be circular in section or rectangular. In either case it must be reduced first by sawing or planing to a rectangular block just over the height and width of your plasticine model.

2 The side profile of the head is drawn on each side of the wooden block, and the point of the nose, the most prominent feature, marked in a line across the front of the block. The grain direction of the wood runs from the top of the head to the base of the neck.

3 The block is now placed in the vice with the face surface upwards for the cutting to begin.

4 Two broad planes can now be cut using a wide chisel and mallet. The mallet should strike the shaft of the chisel in a series of sharp taps rather than with great blows. In this way there is more control over the chisel's direction, and less chance of dislodging the wood from its fixed position. If the cutting angle at the edge of the chisel is upwards, the chisel tends to curve into the wood, and if the chisel is turned with the cutting angle below, then the cutting direction curves upwards. You may remove the surface area from nose to neck first, then work in the opposite direction following the grain of the wood from nose to forehead.

5 All the angles of the features in profile are now chiselled out, turning the chisel round where necessary to follow the grain direction.

6 The head is now reversed in the vice and the profile of the back of the head is cut.

7 The head is turned sideways in the vice. To protect the nose and back of the head, the block must be padded with folded rag where it comes in contact with the metal. The sides of the head from ear to neck in one direction, and from ear to crown of the head in the other are cleared.

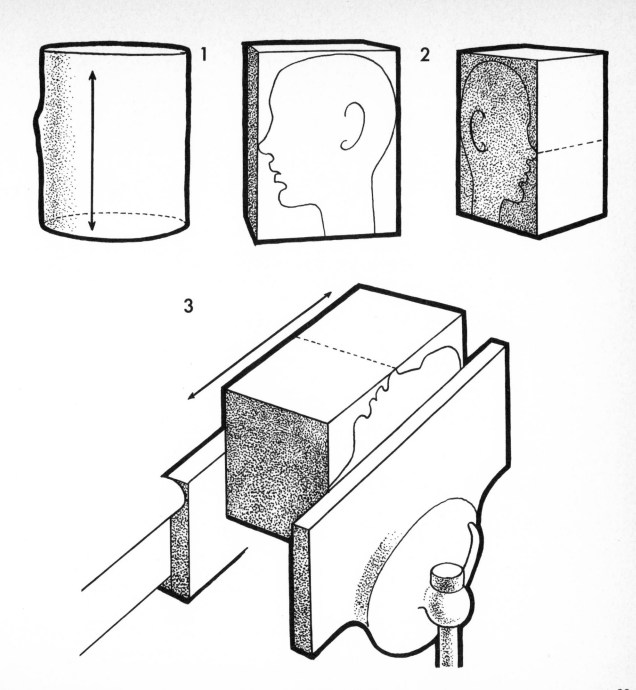

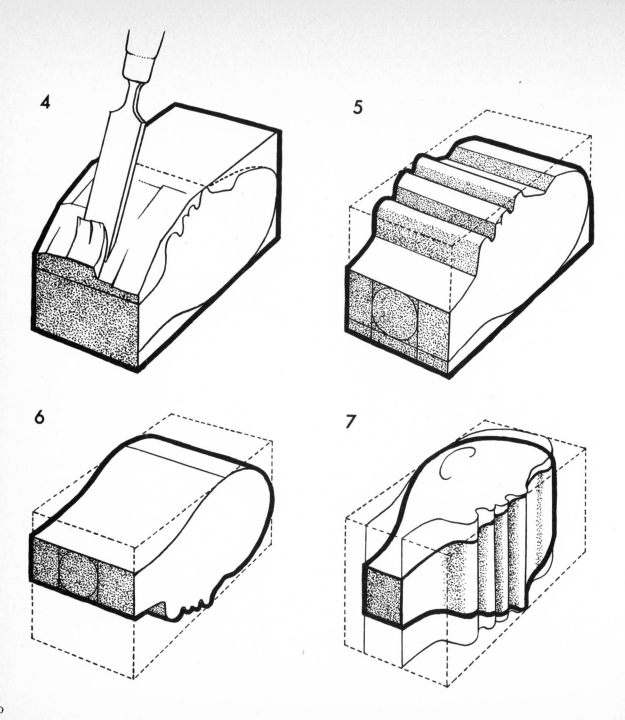

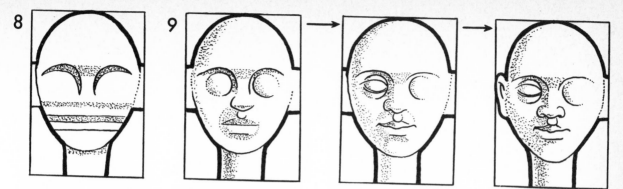

8 Holding the head in the vice between the ears, the lines of the brows above the eyes leading to the bridge of the nose are cut out with a small chisel.

9 From this stage onwards the head may be fixed in a carver's screw or held in a cloth in the hand. You may continue to work with a chisel or use a file to round the top of the head, cheeks and chin. Using a small chisel with the hand only, details of eye sockets, mouth, nose and lastly ears are cut. The surface may be left with the chisel marks intact, or filed and sand-papered smooth.

Hands for glove puppets, and hands and feet for marionettes are carved using the same basic principles. Profiles of both may be traced from the plans of wooden puppets in the section on marionettes which follows.

The neck of a wooden head for a glove puppet must be drilled hollow to fit the index finger and if necessary a cardboard tube can extend its length within the glove. Hands carved in wood must also be attached to cardboard tubes to fit the thumb and third finger of the manipulator.

Painting and hair

Oil paint thinned with turpentine is the most useful paint for *papier maché* and wooden puppets. The surface when dry is smooth without being slimy, and it is also washable. Acrylic paints and waterproof poster paint are also suitable.

Before paint is applied the surface of both *papier maché* and wooden puppets must be prepared. *Papier maché* can be sealed with a coat of thin varnish to prevent paint from being entirely absorbed. Wood must be sealed also and frequently a patent grain filler is used. With the small areas of wood involved in puppetry however, I find it quite sufficient to rub in ground white oil paint with a finger. When this is dry the final tinted coat can be applied.

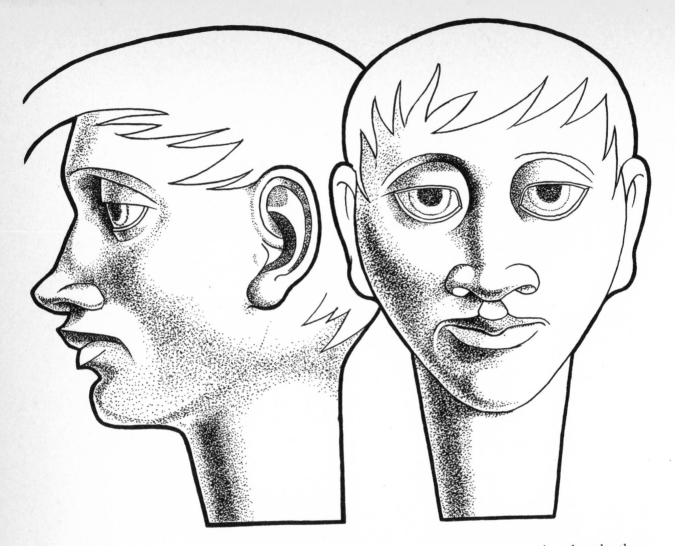

In painting the faces of puppets it is important to remember that the three-dimensional modelling of the features is the most important means of suggesting character under stage lighting. The painted colour and line of eyes and mouth are better suggested than sharply defined.

Hair may be included in the carving of wooden puppets or in the modelling of *papier maché* heads. Where hair must be added, real hair can be glued to the head in cut lengths starting at the outer edges of the scalp. Each section overlaps the previous one until the centre parting is reached. Fur and lambs wool can also be used with the suede side glued on to the puppet's head.

Assembling the head and hands of a glove puppet with a body made from blanket material

Marionettes for a nativity play

44

Marionettes

Marionettes are puppets worked by strings from above, and are the most ambitious attempt in puppetry of the portrayal of the whole human figure. These puppets were introduced into England from Italy in the second half of the seventeenth century and rapidly became more popular than the traditional glove puppet which survived mostly in the form of Punch and Judy. At the same time the material for puppet plays developed from folk lore sources into much more sophisticated dramatic productions.

Marionettes are probably the most difficult to make and to control of all puppets, as the mechanism is comparatively remote from the figure. There can be various grades of difficulty in making marionettes, but I would never advise a beginner in puppetry to tackle even the easiest until he has had some experience with rod or glove puppet making.

Marionettes may be made of *papier maché*, cloth or wood. Whatever the material careful planning is important, and some understanding of the function and proportions of the human body is essential for good design. I have added here comparative charts of human anatomy translated into terms of the marionette for guidance.

The height of marionettes may vary considerably. Usually they are not less than $1\frac{1}{2}$ ft. and not more than 3 ft. The movements of very small marionettes are not visible at any great distance, and with larger marionettes, the weight becomes unwieldy.

Proportions of the body

In designing a puppet, it is helpful to have some idea of the general proportions of the figure. Sometimes distortion or exaggeration adds to character, but this should be consciously done.

Too often the head is mistakenly tackled first by a beginner making a puppet, and the height and proportions thought of later. This may lead to the head and hands being far too large for the rest of the body. Now this may not matter in the case of glove puppets where the overall length is undefined; but the marionette expresses itself with the whole body, not the head alone. When too much emphasis is given to one part, the significance of the movements as a whole are lost. A head is seldom more than one-seventh of the complete body height in an adult, and a scale drawing should be made of the whole puppet before work begins on any one part.

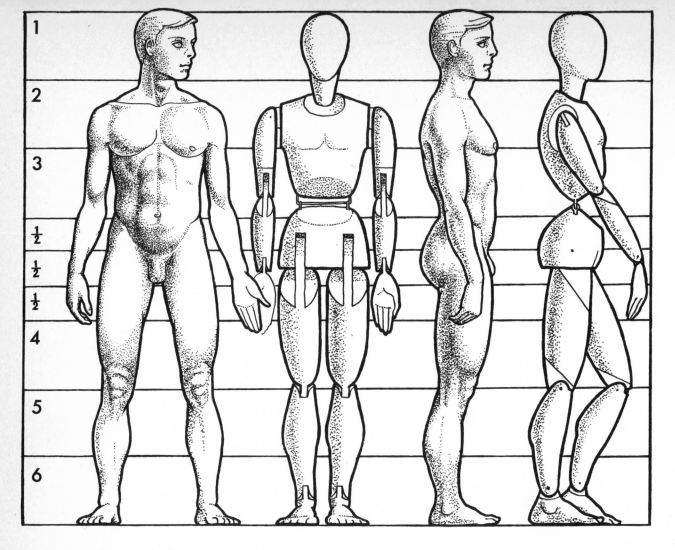

Proportions of the male figure

The head is usually taken as a unit of measurement, and in the average male figure there are seven and a half units in the complete height. The following points may be remembered and noted in the diagrams:

a The division of the legs is at the mid-height level of the body.

b The elbow joint is level with the waist.

c The shoulders are two units wide; the hips one and a half units.

d The arm divides into three units—armpit to elbow, elbow to wrist and wrist to finger tips.

46

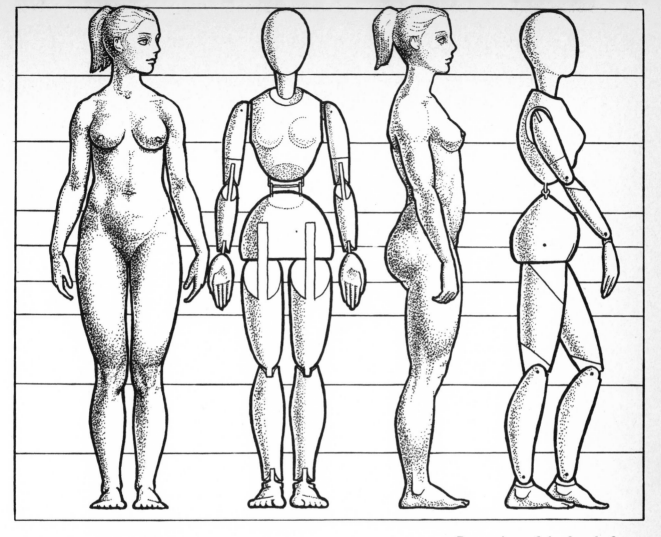

Proportions of the female figure

e The hand is the length of the chin to hairline.
f The feet are slightly more than one unit long.

The female figure is more variable than the male, but the following comparisons
are usually true.

a The shoulders are narrower and more sloping.
b The hips are wider.
c The waist is narrower.
d The legs are proportionately shorter, altering the line of mid-height.

47

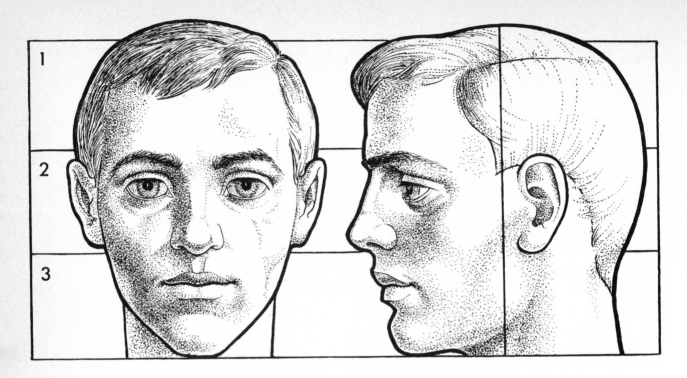

Proportions of the head

Just as the head, hands and feet, are parts of the complete figure, so the features of the head are related to each other. In looking at the average head, we should remember that a slight deviation of one feature from the normal can be more telling than a set of exaggerated features, each one crowding for attention.

Seen from the front, the head may be divided horizontally into three equal sections.

1 From the top of the skull to the brow line
2 From the brow to the base of the nose
3 From the base of the nose to the chin

The mouth is placed a little above the middle of the lowest section. The ears lie within the limits of the centre section. The distance between the eyes is the width of one eye.

Seen from the side the head may be divided vertically in two. The ear lies behind the centre division. The eye is set well back in its socket from the bridge of the nose. This distance may be as much as the width of the base of the nose.

Cloth marionettes

Cloth marionettes are most easily made from stuffed stocking material, which can be stretched, drawn in with sewing, or filled out with stuffing as the shape demands. A thick nylon stocking makes a very good head and body for a cloth marionette.

Starting from the top, the head is made from the heel padded into a sphere with the toe of the foot cut off, and the neck is gathered and tightly sewn below it. The upper part of the body should have a piece of dowelling running between the shoulders which is used for string attachments taking the weight of the whole puppet. The waist joint is a hinge formed by a double row of sewing. The lower half of the body is cut and sewn straight across. Some lead shot or sheet lead for weight should be placed in this part to make the body hang straight when in use.

In a small cloth marionette, limbs can also be made from stocking material sewn into tubing. A tightly bound round division gives a freely moving joint, and straight across sewing makes a hinge joint. With larger marionettes lengths of dowelling make good arms and legs covered with a sleeve of material. These pieces of wood are sawn or filed to an angle for hinge joints at knee or elbow, and held in place by sewing across the hinge. At shoulder, wrist, thigh and ankle the ends are filed round.

Legs are sewn on to the lower half of the body with a hinge joint, and a free-moving shoulder joint is sewn to the upper part of the body, or pinned to the piece of cross dowelling.

Hands and feet are best cut in felt and in a cloth marionette there is little to be gained in any movement at wrist and ankle joints. The face can simply be coloured in with chalk and sprayed with a fixing fluid, or a *papier maché* mask can be pasted on. For beginners it is always possible to buy dolls' faces from a craft shop. Hair can be made from lengths of wool or thread sewn through the head and knotted in groups to remain in place.

The completed cloth marionette can be strung in a simple version of the stringing for the wooden marionette demonstrated at the end of this section.

Papier maché marionettes

It would be possible to model each part of a marionette in plasticine, make plaster moulds and cast the head, body and limbs in *papier maché*. Provided that wire loops were threaded through the limbs for joints and string attachments, the whole marionette could be assembled and strung in the usual way. However, the work in this method would be endless. The most successful *papier maché* puppet is made by direct modelling.

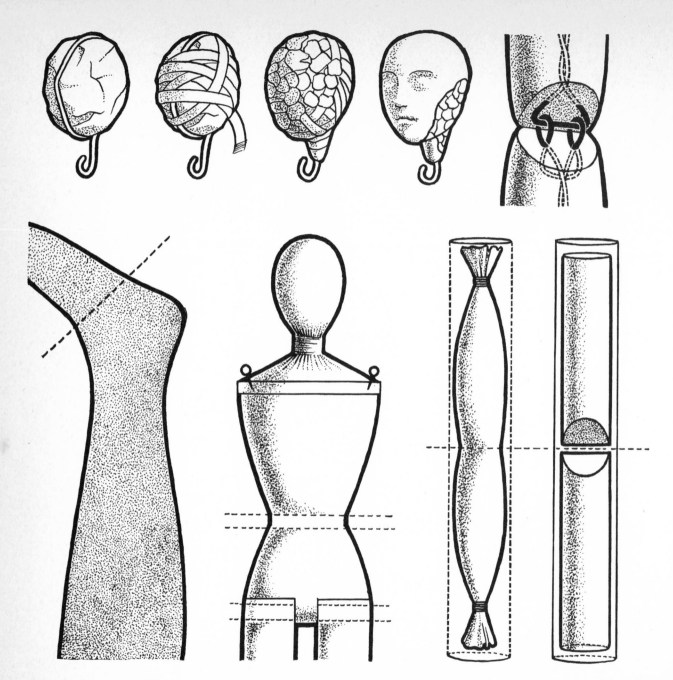

Cloth and *papier maché* marionettes

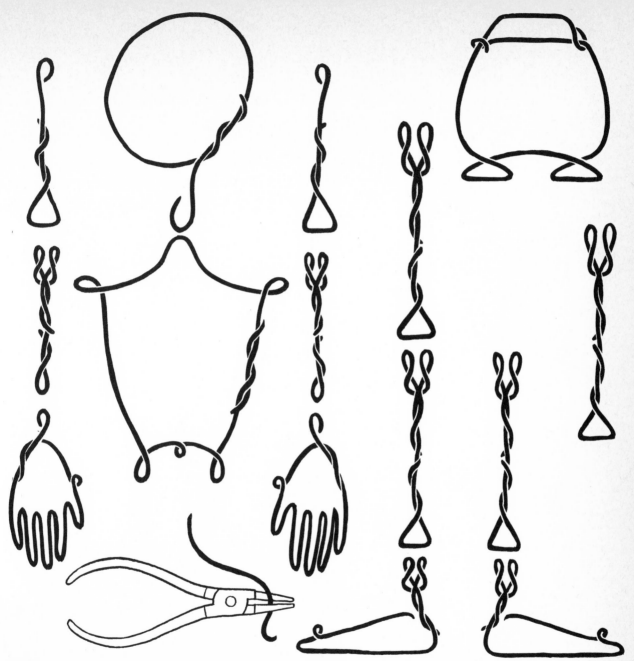

Wire framework for a *papier maché* marionette

The diagram in this section shows a suggested wire framework for a *papier maché* marionette. For convenience in copying I have drawn the parts separately but before modelling begins the parts should all be interlocked, except for head and hands which can be attached later. The drawings of the building up of the head show the method used for all parts of the body. The wire frame is either filled or surrounded with newspaper soaked in size. The whole part is bound tightly with bandaging. A further layer of laminated *papier maché* begins to suggest features, and a final layer of *papier maché* pulp brings the modelling to a finish. When this layer is dry it can be sand-papered smooth, and sealed with thin spirit varnish ready for painting.

Screw eyes for string attachments cannot be used with *papier maché*, and loops for stringing must be included in the wire framework. Where this is not possible wire loops must be bedded with extra glue in the *papier maché* while it is still wet.

The hinge joints at knee and elbow must be limited in movement by the shape of the modelling. The joints at neck, shoulder and wrist are freely moving.

Wooden marionettes

The parts of the body

The carving of a wooden head and hands has already been described. In principle, the carving of the feet and parts of the body are exactly the same, provided you have a front and side profile clearly marked on your block of wood. I have given diagrams of both a male and female wooden marionette of just over $1\frac{1}{2}$ ft. high as a guide for drawing these profiles.

Although head, hands and feet are cut in close-grained hard wood because of the detail involved, all the parts of the body may be carved from soft wood which is much easier to work. The grain direction of the whole wooden marionette is vertical from head to ankle, the exception being the feet where the grain direction is horizontal. The carving of the parts of the body may be done with a mallet and chisel, or a spokeshave, but an electric sander works very quickly through soft wood. This cannot strictly be called carving, but it saves a lot of time.

If your marionette is to be clothed entirely except for hands, head and feet, there is no reason at all why you should not use wooden dowelling for the legs and arms. I have found $\frac{3}{4}$ in. dowelling for legs and $\frac{1}{2}$ in. dowelling for arms quite suitable. If the weight of the completed marionette is too great, holes can be bored through from front to back of thorax and pelvis, or these parts may be sawn in two and hollowed out with a chisel.

The plans given are of two marionettes carved for a nativity play. They are only 1½ ft. high as the play had a large cast and was presented on a 6-ft. wide stage. Real hair was used for the shepherdess, and a piece of goatskin was soaked and moulded to be glued on the head of the shepherd.

It is by no means necessary to use one type of joint throughout the whole marionette. I prefer string jointing for shoulder and elbow and tongue and groove for knee and ankle joints. It is best to be guided by what is most suitable for the particular movements required by individual puppets. In the instructions of the different types of joint, I have given the example which is most typical of its kind, although there are variations within each type of joint. Some types of waist joint belong to none of the varieties above, but are dealt with in their place in the plans of the wooden marionette. If a joint is well made, it should, like the stringing, be an acceptable part of the whole design. Some people cover joints with thin *chamois* leather painted flesh colour. This is a matter of individual taste.

Joints

The joints of wooden puppets imitate where possible the joint movements of the human body. These may be either hinged joints as seen in the elbow, knee and ankle, or more freely rotating joints as at the neck, shoulder and wrist. An exception is the hip joint. A sideways as well as forward and backward movement of the thigh detracts too much from the stability of the marionette, and this joint is usually cut as a hinge.

There are three principal ways of jointing a wooden puppet—string joints, leather joints and tongue and groove joints cut in the wood of the limbs themselves. I have arranged them in order of difficulty.

String joints are the most flexible type of jointing, and are best used where movement is to be sideways as well as forward and backwards. A combined string jointing at shoulder and elbow makes for excellent arm movement with the ability to move across the front of the body. This is not easily accomplished by any other type of jointing. Sometimes a free-moving waist joint is made, using strong cord which can be continued upwards to make the neck joint. I am not very happy however about string jointing where there is any weight below the joint, and string jointing is not suitable for the more rigid hinge joint of the knee.

Leather joints make a very good hinge where movement is forward or backwards only. Good examples of this are the knee, elbow and ankle joint. Where a more freely moving joint is wanted, leather is less successful. It can be used for the shoulder joint, though I prefer other types of jointing here, and also for the waist joint if no great sideways movement is wanted. The leather used must be strong and supple. For very small puppets *chamois* leather is sufficient, but for larger puppets men's gloving leather is best, or even book-binders' morocco. Hide and calf are too thick and not flexible enough.

Tongue and groove joints are the most difficult joints to make. A carpenter would more correctly name them flexible saddle joints. These joints give a more natural appearance than other types of jointing, and give the satisfaction of meeting a technical challenge. In the plans of the two wooden marionettes which follow, I have shown tongue and groove joints with their variations throughout as they need to be most carefully planned. I often cut profiles in card of tongue and groove joints, and rotate them around a pin to see what range of movement I may have. The tongue and groove joints in the following instructions are stopped on one side so that movement is in one direction only. This is the most complicated tongue and groove joint to make and it is used at the elbow and knee.

Making a string joint

Tools needed: bench saw, hand drill, file.

a Two saw cuts remove a little over half of each end to be jointed. When the two ends are fitted together there is a narrow vertical space between them. The first cut is made with the wood fixed in a vice, the second on a bench hook.

b A hole is drilled through the centre of each projecting tongue at the joint ends. These are best drilled separately, fixed with a 'G' cramp over a piece of waste wood. An opening for the drill is first made with a sharp pointed tool.

c The projecting tongues at the joint ends are filed or sand-papered round.

d String is passed through the drilled holes from one side to the other of the joint. Inside the joint the space between the tongues is loosely strung, and the outside ends of the string are knotted and cut close. It is always safer to paint the finished knots with glue. The string used must vary with the size of your puppet, and must be strong enough to take the weight of the lower limb of the joint. *Macramé* twine makes a rather large knot, but lasts a long time without fraying. The cord in string joints must be renewed from time to time.

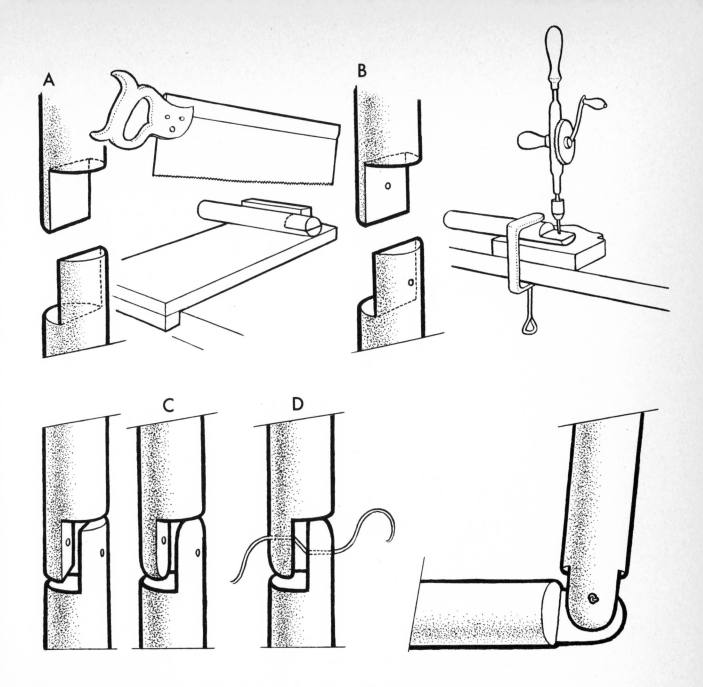

Making a string joint

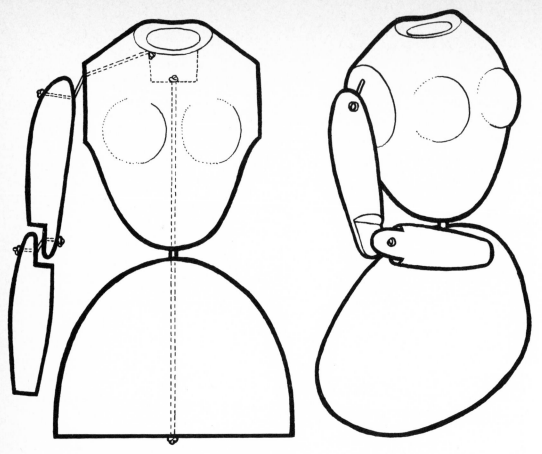

Some useful string joints

Making a leather joint

Tools needed: bench saw, file, razor blade, hammer.

a A straight saw cut is made down the centre of each part to be jointed. These saw cuts should be exactly opposite each other. The cut made should be of the same thickness as the leather which is to be used, so for small joints with *chamois* leather a hacksaw is sufficient. For larger joints with thicker leather a tenon saw makes a wider cut.

b One half of each part to be jointed is filed to an angle. This may be done with a chisel if you prefer. The degree of the angle controls the range of movement in the finished joint.

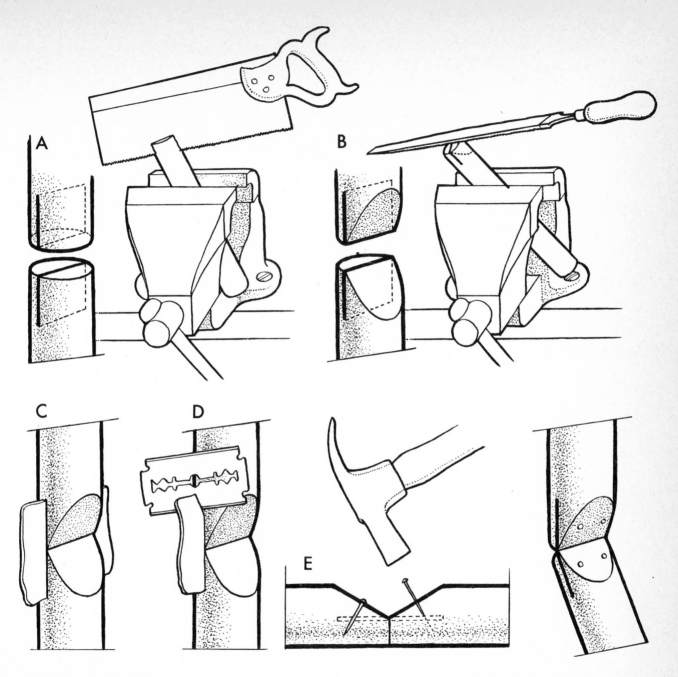

Making a leather joint

c A square cut piece of leather is eased into each groove in turn, until the two halves of the joint fit closely together. A little glue is run into the bottom of each groove but kept clear of the joint ends.

d The overlapping leather is trimmed with a razor blade close to the sides of the joint.

e After testing movement to make sure that the joint is not too tight, two small pins are tapped into each filed surface of the joint to pierce and fix the leather. Picture framer's pins are best for this purpose. If they are too long they can be cut with wire cutters, and driven in with the cut end lying across the grain of the wood.

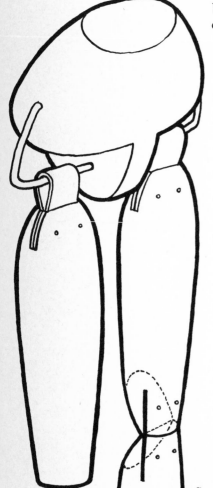

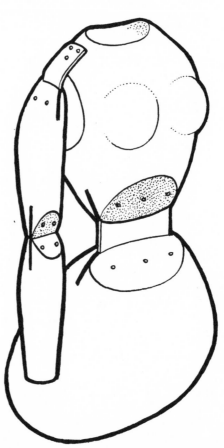

Some useful leather joints

Making a tongue and groove joint

Tools needed: bench saw, mallet and chisel, file, hand-drill, wire cutters and round-nosed pliers.

a Two vertical saw cuts in the end of each part to be jointed are made opposite each other. These saw cuts divide the end surfaces into three equal sections. In the upper part to be jointed, two further side cuts remove each outer third, leaving a shoulder lying at an angle. The angle of the shoulder helps determine the range of movement in the finished joint.

b The lower part to be jointed has the centre third chiselled out at the angle shown. Use a chisel of the same width as the groove to be cut.

c A small notch is cut from the short side of the tongue, and the groove in the lower part of the joint is deepened to allow the tongue to fit.

d The end of the tongue is filed round, and the surfaces of the lower half of the joint are also rounded.

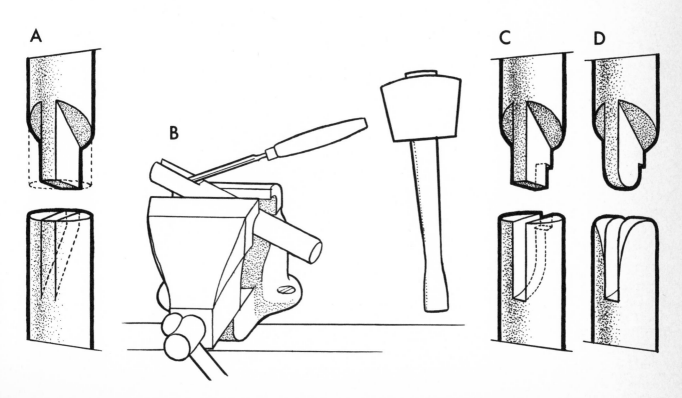

e The tongue and groove are fitted into each other. If they are tight they are better left so at present; if slack then the joint should be wedged with paper to keep it in position for the hand-drill. While you are using the drill the joint may be held in position by a 'G' cramp over a piece of waste wood, or you may ask someone to hold it in position for you. The size of the drill bit should be the same as the wire to be used in fixing the joint.

f Make sure that the tongue can move easily in its groove. If the fit is too tight, the sides of the groove must be cleared further with a chisel. A short length of wire is inserted through the joint, cut, and turned over at each end to form a loop too wide to slip back into the shaft.

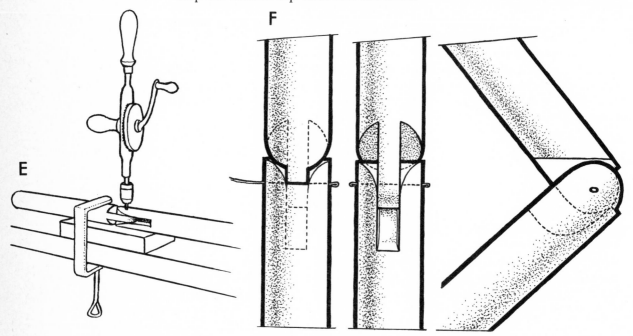

Making a tongue and groove joint

Plans for two wooden marionettes

Neck joint The base of the neck is attached to the base of a socket in the thorax by means of two cup hooks which are closed with pliers when in place. The socket is most neatly made by a brace and $\frac{3}{4}$-in. bit, and widened slightly at the top with a chisel used sideways to the grain direction. The movements at this joint are forwards, backward and sideways, limited by the rim of the socket.

Waist joint There are many variations to this joint, but I prefer those made with thick wire passed through large screw eyes and fitted into drilled channels in the woodwork. If the opening in the screw eye is larger than the thickness of the wire there is a certain amount of sideways movement as well as the forward and backward hinge movement. A metal hinge joint gives no sideways movement, and a string joint possibly too much, but this will depend on the actions necessary to the performance of your marionette.

Shoulder joint The shoulder joint shown here is rather complicated to make and is used with upper arm rotation. In most cases I much prefer a string joint at shoulder and elbow, but this more complicated joint has the advantage that the shape of the shoulder is preserved whatever the movement may be. A housing for a short piece of ½-in. dowelling is drilled into the thorax at shoulder level. One half of the piece of dowelling is cut into a tongue to fit the groove of the upper arm. The other half of the dowelling has a groove filed round it. A small length of thick wire or very fine dowelling is passed through the top of the socket in the thorax, and lies in the groove of the dowel, holding it in place but allowing rotation.

Wrist joint This is an open tongue and groove joint. The tongue is most easily cut as a separate piece of wood and glued into a socket in the hand. Variations of the wrist joint show a wire and screw eye mechanism which allows some sideways movement.

Hip joint There are many variations of this joint. The tongue and groove joint closed at the back of the pelvis probably has the best appearance and control in the walking movement. A screw eye and wire attachment allows a slight sideways movement, and the screw attachment of legs at an angle to the sides of the pelvis allows an outward splay when the knee is raised which can be amusing if wanted. A complete sideways movement at the hip is seldom attempted as the walking movement becomes impossible to control.

Knee joint This is a straightforward closed hinge joint.

Ankle joint The variations in the ankle joint are of appearance rather than function, as all that is needed is a limited hinge joint. The amount of drop allowed to the foot may be controlled by the stringing, or by the shape of the joint itself. In all constructions of the foot and ankle it is necessary to attach the foot at an angle slightly outwards from the shaft of the leg to avoid the risk of the feet getting in each others' way when walking. It is sometimes necessary also to add weight to the front sole of the foot to make it drop when the knee is raised. A small piece of sheet lead is suitable for this.

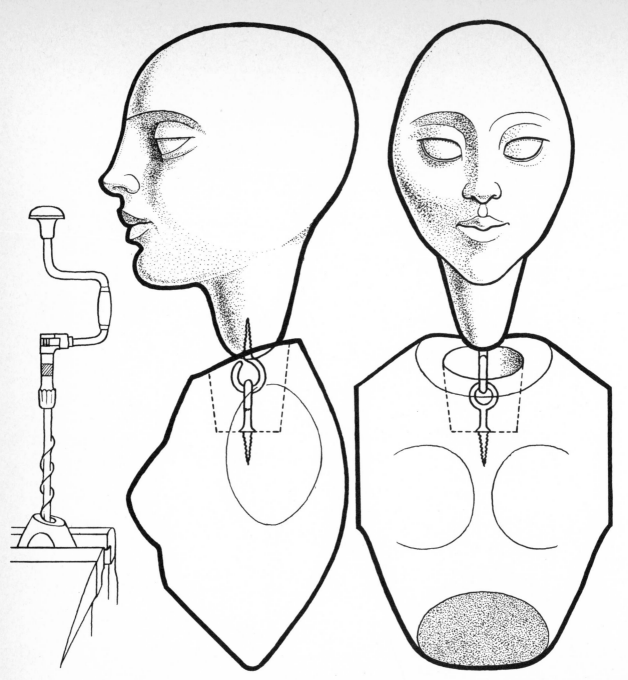

Head, thorax and neck joint

62

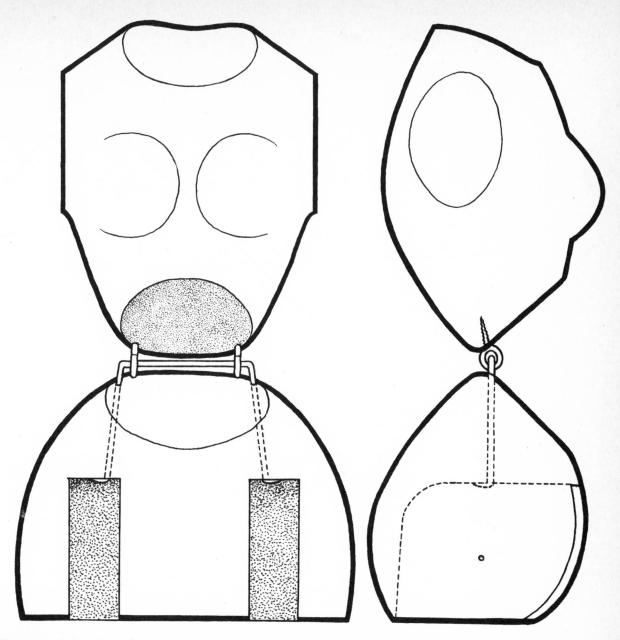

Thorax, pelvis and waist joint

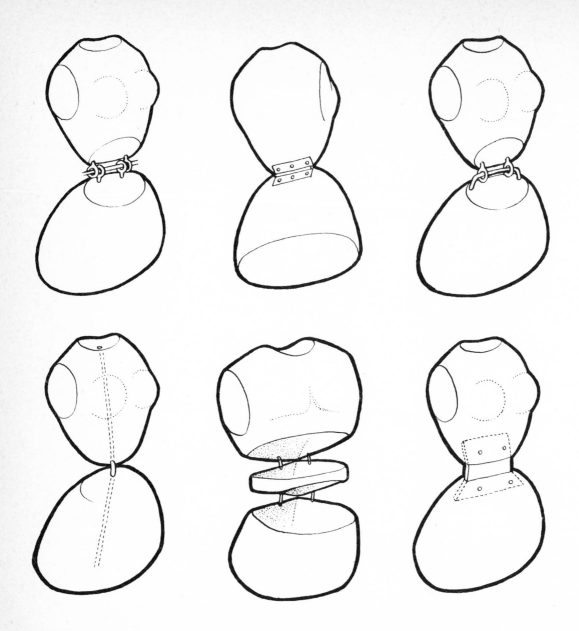

Alternative waist joints

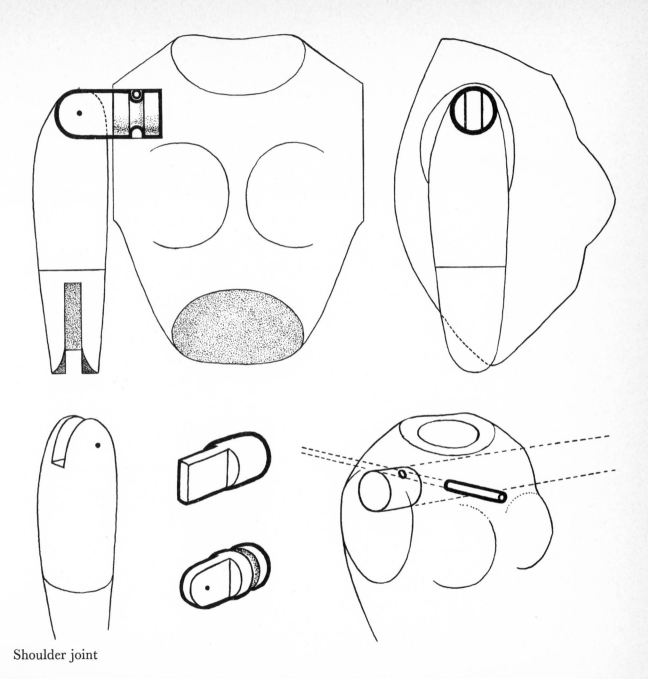

Shoulder joint

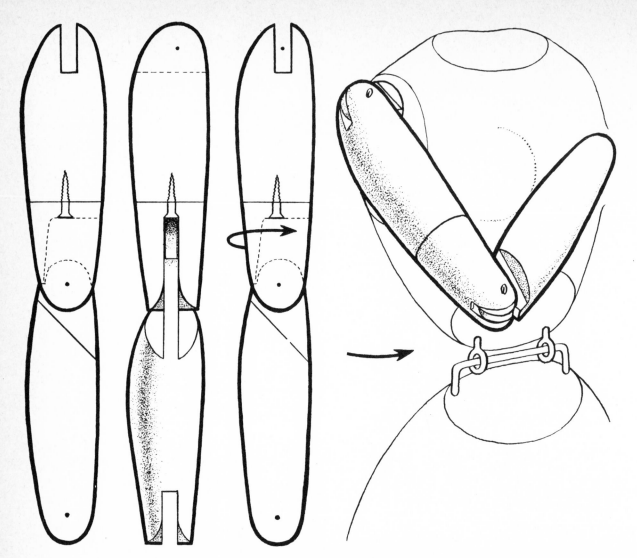

Upper arm rotation This movement is combined with a closed hinge joint at the elbow and allows the arm to move across the front of the body. The upper arm is cut into two, at a distance above the groove of the elbow joint equal to the unthreaded part of the screw shaft. The thread of the screw is fixed firmly in the upper part of the arm, and the lower part of the screw passes freely through a shaft drilled from the groove of the elbow allowing a circling movement.

32398

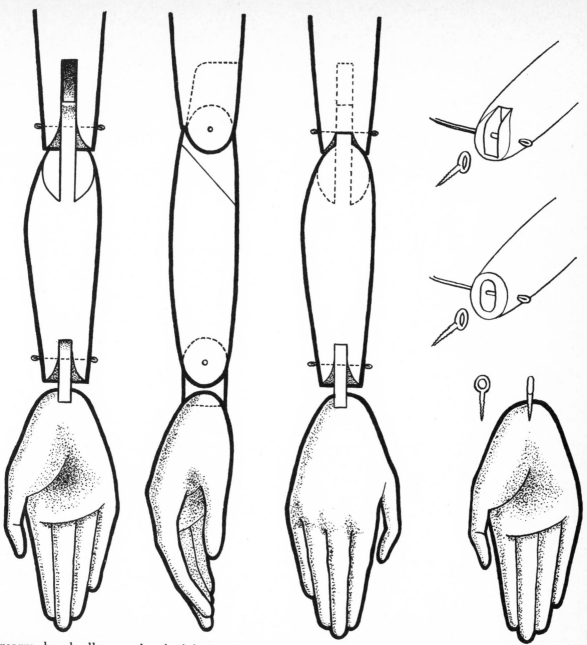

Forearm, hand, elbow and wrist joints

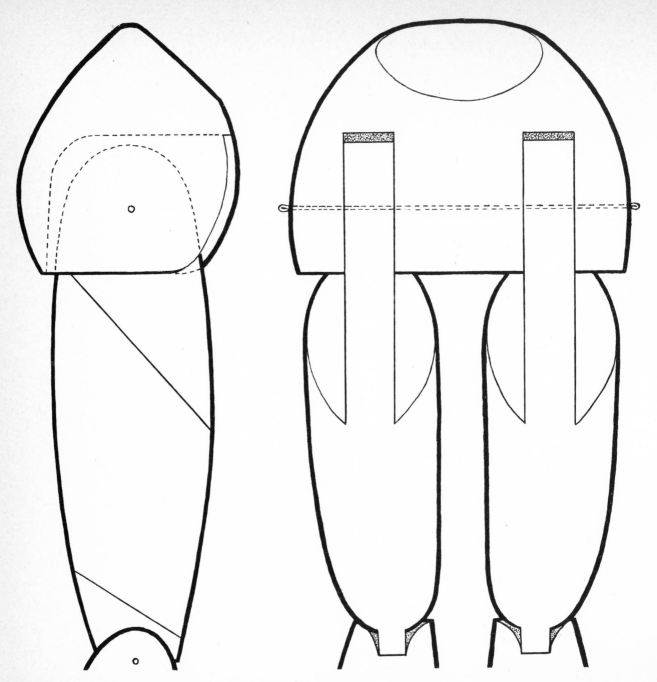

Pelvis, thigh and hip joint

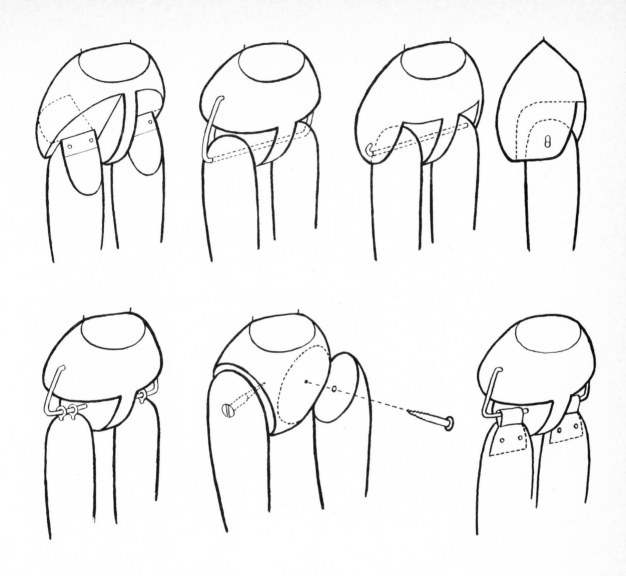

Alternative hip joints

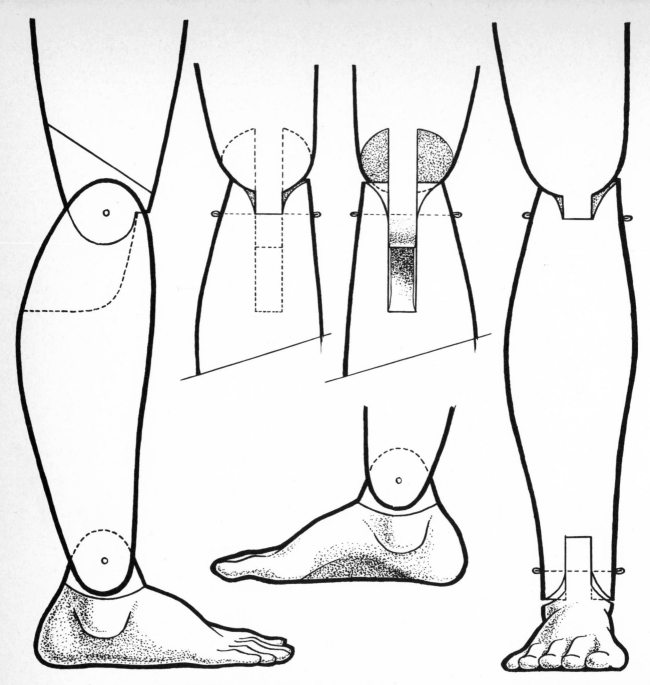

Lower leg, foot, knee and ankle joints

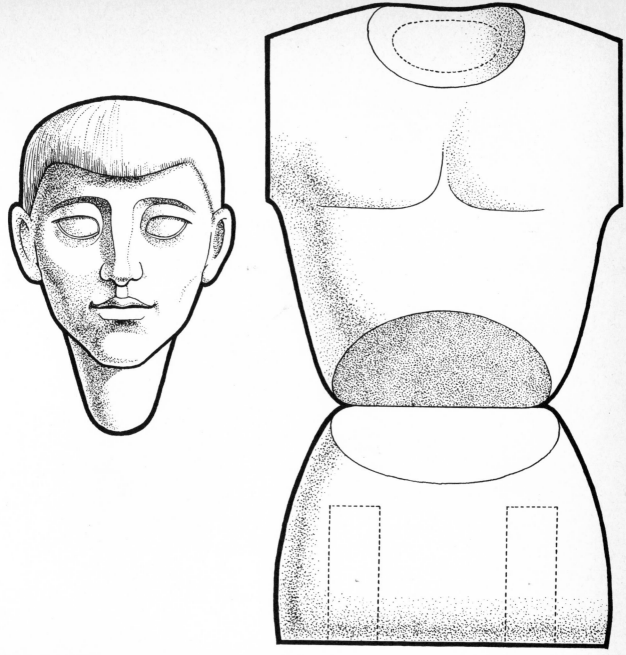

Parts of the shepherd marionette. Actual size. Front view

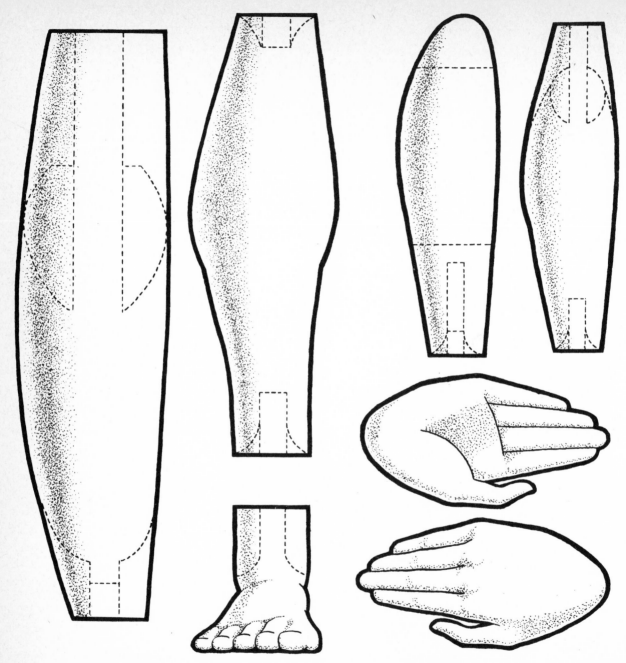

Parts of the shepherd marionette. Actual size. Front view.

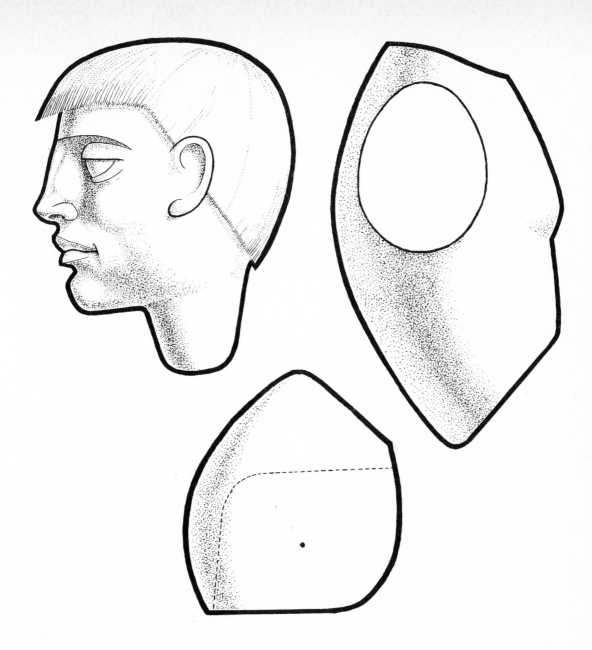

Parts of the shepherd marionette. Actual size. Side view

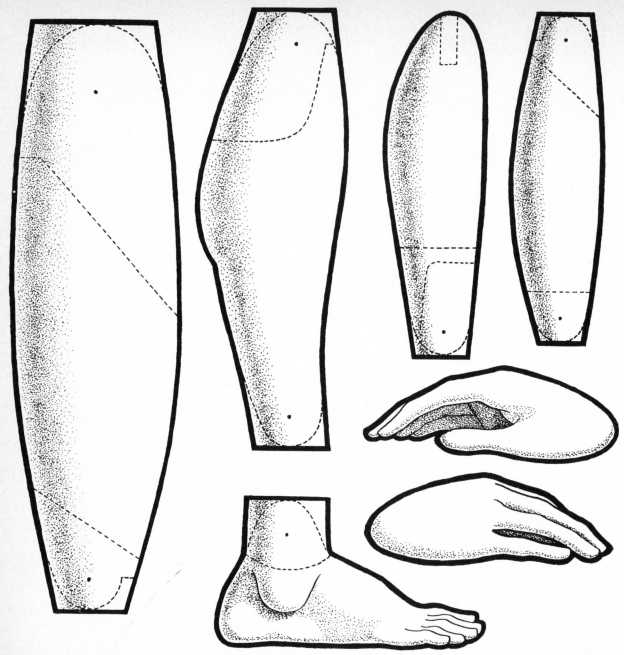

Parts of the shepherd marionette. Actual size. Side view

Controls

The mechanism for moving the strings of the marionette is known as the control bar, crutch or perch. There are two main types—the vertical control bar and the horizontal control bar. The vertical control is most commonly used in Europe, and the horizontal in America, and there are advantages and disadvantages in both.

Vertical control bar In any type of control there are two groups of movement—those made by altering the position of the whole mechanism and those made by detaching a part of the controls and working it separately. In the vertical control bar shown here, the hand bar is detachable for separate movement with one hand. The other hand holds the main mechanism, and operates the walking movement by means of the thumb insertion in the swivel walking bar. I have found this a fairly effective balance for work.

The thumb mechanism in the walking bar is not equally effective with either hand, and it may be removed if you prefer it leaving a narrow light swivel bar which can be raised alternately on either side by the forward projecting thumb and index finger.

Some people prefer to use a detachable bar for the walking movement, keeping the hand strings attached to the main control bar on a running string which is looped through screw eyes without being knotted.

Horizontal control bar This type of control shows a detachable walking bar held separately from the main mechanism when in use. The hands are on a running string through a screw eye at the front of the controls.

Although I prefer the walking movement in the vertical control bar, the head movements in the horizontal control are better defined. A strip of leather or tape can be fixed from one end of the top of the horizontal bar to the other across the back of the hand to safeguard it from being dropped.

For four-legged animal movement a type of horizontal control bar is always used. Other types of control are not typical and are usually designed for particular movements in a particular marionette. This is a matter for experiment.

Either type of control bar is quite easily made. A broom handle gives enough wood for several vertical control bars, with the addition of narrow dowelling for the bowing string attachment. The walking bar and head string attachment can be cut from plywood. The horizontal control bar may be entirely cut from plywood with narrow dowelling for the bowing string and shoulder attachments. Washers must be used in the screwing of swivel bars. Other attachments are pinned and glued into spaces drilled or chiselled to house them.

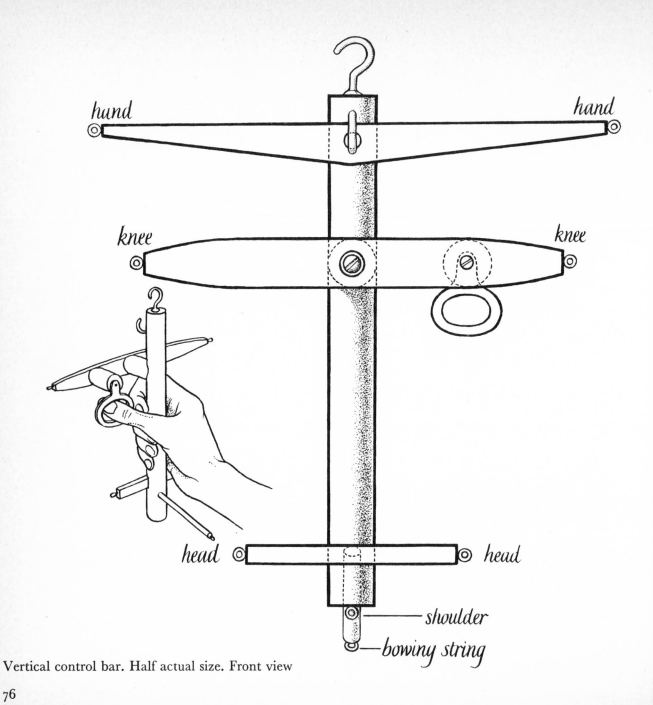

hand · hand · knee · knee · head · head · shoulder · bowing string

Vertical control bar. Half actual size. Front view

76

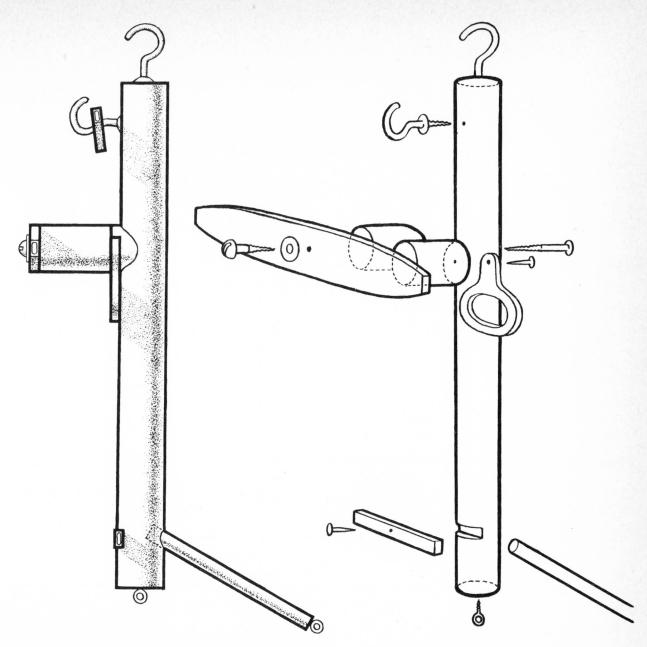

Vertical control bar. Half actual size. Side view

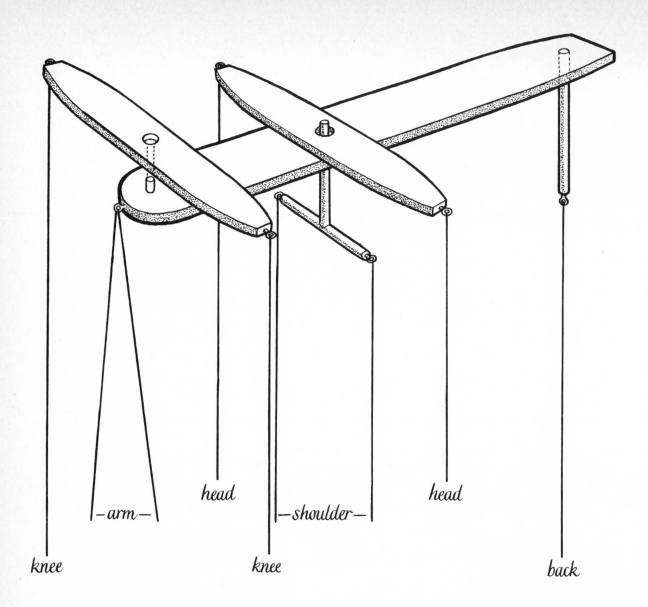

knee

–arm–

head

–shoulder–

knee

head

back

Horizontal control bar. Half actual size

Stringing

Strings used for marionettes may vary in thickness from *macramé* twine to fine carpet thread. The size and weight of the marionette must guide your choice. I have never felt it to be of great importance that stringing should be invisible, as strings may well be considered an acceptable part of the marionette design. If you do prefer not to see stringing, dark colours show less than light, and fishing twine is very thin, but strong at the same time.

The length of the strings depends on various factors—the height of the marionette, the size and type of control bar, the distance between the leaning rail and stage floor, and the actions that the marionette is to perform. The marionettes shown in these pages are 20 in. high with a vertical control bar, and the leaning rail of the theatre for which they were designed is $5\frac{1}{2}$ ft. above the stage floor. The head and shoulder strings are 4 ft. long, and the longest strings not more than $5\frac{1}{2}$ ft. I found this height sufficient for walking and sitting movements, and the controls could not be seen from the front row. For lying down movements longer strings would be necessary.

In wooden marionettes, strings are attached to small screw-eyes fixed in appropriate positions in the control bar, and in the marionette itself. Screw-eyes cannot be used in *papier maché* however, and in *papier maché* puppet construction, wire loops must be included in the framework.

All the strings apart from those to the head, hands and feet may have to be passed through clothing. I prefer to complete the stringing before clothing so that I can see exactly what is happening in trial movements and adjustments. Later, the strings can be untied at the control end, passed through the clothing beside the attachment points of the body, and then retied to the control bar.

Before starting to attach the strings, the control bar is hung from a free standing hook at the height you have measured for the length of your stringing. The strings are then tied in place in the following order:

1 *Shoulder strings* The shoulder strings are attached first, as they take the main weight of the body in all movements. The strings run from one screw-eye at the base of the shaft of the control bar to screw-eyes just within the shoulder joint edge of the upper half of the body. Since these two strings have a common origin, sideways or forward tilting of the control bar has little effect on the marionette and stability and support are maintained. These strings must be tied evenly so that the shoulders hang level and the marionette's feet are just raised from the floor. All other strings are measured and adjusted in relation to the shoulder strings and must be tied carefully so as not to alter the tautness of the

first stringing. If the joints at neck, waist, hip, knee and ankle are designed to lie exactly below each other in one line, then the marionette will hang from the shoulder strings in a natural standing pose. A well designed marionette should be able to support a little of its own weight in a standing position, should the manipulator's arm become tired.

2 *Head strings* The head strings run from either side of the lower cross piece on the control bar to just above the ear on either side of the head. The screw-eyes in the head are placed so that the balance of weight is slightly to the front. When the supporting strings are relaxed the head then falls forward. This is important in nodding and head turning movements.

3 *Bowing string* This string runs from the tip of the backward projecting rod on the controls, and is attached to the base of the thorax at the back. It should be taut, but not taut enough to pull the straight hanging position of the marionette out of line.

4 *Knee strings* The knee strings run from either side of the knee cross piece on the controls to screw-eyes fitted just above the front of each knee joint. These strings must be really taut, even to the point of slightly bending the joint, so that any movement of the knee bar has instant response.

5 *Foot strings* These strings run from the screw-eyes already fixed above the knee joints to the centre front of the feet. Foot strings must be slack to allow a natural drop of the foot when the knee is raised, but not so slack as to let the feet drag. The feet are weighted at the bottom to help this movement.

6 *Hand strings* I usually attach these strings with the hand bar in position on the crutch. The attachment point on the hand can vary according to the action that is required, but for general use it is best to place the screw-eyes half way along the thumb side of each hand. When the hand bar is raised each hand turns sideways which is more natural than the palm forward position. The hands should be strung slightly raised when the hand bar is in place to avoid a lifeless appearance.

This system of stringing covers a good range of movements. Special effects and movements need special stringing which must be worked out by experiment.

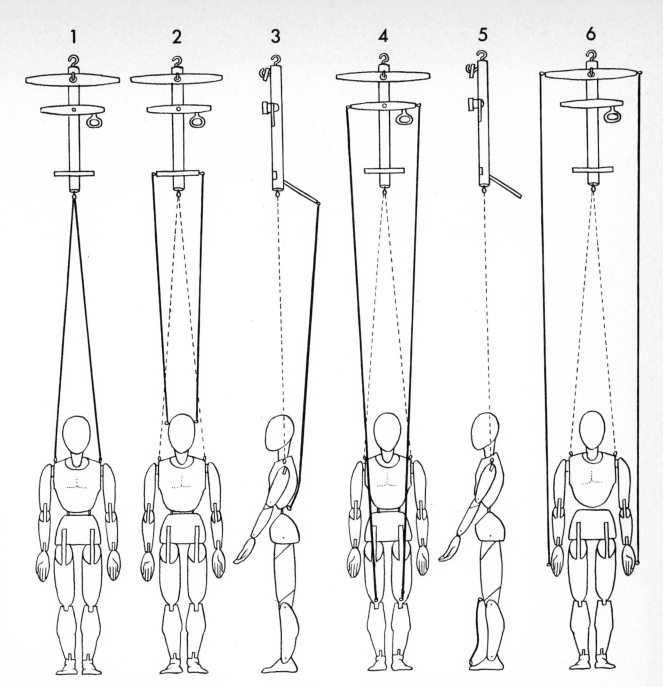

Attaching the strings

Precautions

Tangled strings Through carelessness or bad luck strings can become tangled. If the tangling is recent and not extensive it may be sufficient to hang up the controls to allow the marionette to untwist, and to work through looped strings without undoing any of the string attachments.

If the tangling is tight and knotted the weight of the hanging marionette will only make things worse. In this case lay out the marionette and controls on a table or floor and undo the hand bar attachments. With these removed you have a better chance of straightening the rest of the stringing. The shoulder strings should never be undone or the balance may be altered.

Handling When lifting or carrying a marionette, hold the controls in one hand, and with the other gather the strings together at mid height. With the hands held well apart the puppet will hang clear of the floor and may be lifted over the bar at the side of the stage quite easily.

Storing For short periods marionettes are best stored hanging up to prevent tangling. Over long periods, however, it is better to take the weight off the strings and lay them flat. If tapes are tied round the strings below the control bar, and above the marionette's head the risk of tangled strings is reduced. A small bag or cloak tied at the neck over the marionette protects it from dust and from tangling with others.

The movements of the marionette

Some movements arise from the balance or tilt of the whole control bar, and some from the separate movement of a single string. The following group of movements belong to the first type.

1 *Bowing* This is a very easy movement. The control bar is tilted forward while the point of the bowing string attachment remains level. The slackening of the head and shoulder strings allows the upper part of the body to incline forward, but the support of the bowing string at the base of the thorax keeps the lower half of the body straight from the waist down. If the hand bar is left on its hook, the hands hang forward quite naturally with the palms out.

2 *Head turning* This is a more subtle movement and difficult to do at first. It results from a slight forward and sideways tilt of the control bar. The forward tilt allows the head to fall forward. The sideways tilt slackens one head string, and tightens the other, pulling the head to one side.

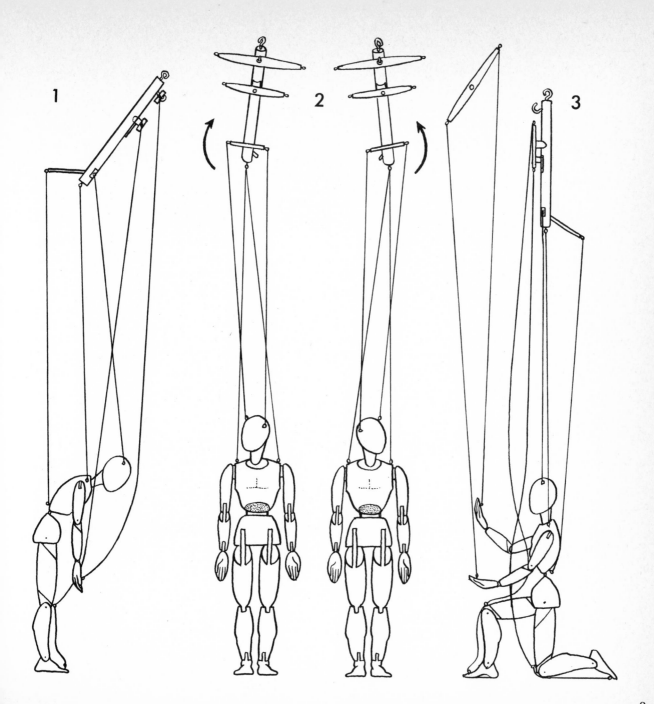

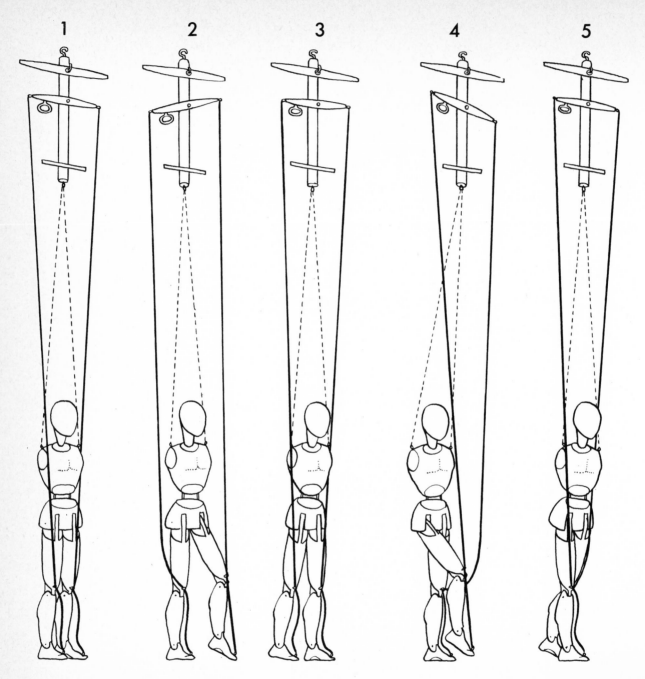

3 *Kneeling on one knee* A downwards movement of the thumb in the knee bar raises and bends the marionette's right leg while the whole crutch is moved forward and lowered. Kneeling on both knees is not so successful, as the forward movement is less controlled and ends with a jerk.

All these movements may be done with one hand only, leaving the other hand free to work the hand bar.

Hand and leg movements belong to the second type of manipulation, where individual strings control the action. Hands are comparatively easy to work. The hand bar may be taken off its hook and used for both hands together, or it may be left in its place and one string for one hand only used at a time. Leg movements are not so easy to control. Not all puppeteers lay equal importance on a walking movement in the marionette. However I feel that a convincing walking movement is important if the marionette is to express itself completely.

4 *Walking*

1 An evenly balanced starting position.
2 The downward movement of the thumb in the knee bar slackens the left string and raises the right knee.
3 The whole control bar moves forward over the right leg which straightens as the knee bar returns to its horizontal position. The left leg closes beside the right partly from weight and partly from the beginning of the next movement.
4 The upward movement of the thumb raises the left knee.
5 The control bar moves forward over the left leg while the right swings forward to close beside the other.

Although walking has to be described in stages, the forward movement of the control bar is flowing and continuous.

The diagram for the walking movement is drawn as it would be seen in a mirror by a right-handed manipulator, for that is the best way to practise. Early trials in walking a new puppet are nearly always disappointing and adjustments have to be made. Usual faults are dragging feet and a side-to-side swinging of the lower half of the body. The following points should be checked in improving the action.

a Knee strings at resting position must be really taut, so that none of the range of movement is wasted in gathering up slack stringing.
b Feet must be well weighted to keep the lower half of the body stable and to make the toes drop naturally when the knee is raised.
c The ankle joints must be constructed so that the feet turn out slightly, and do not catch in passing each other.

d The marionette must never be raised to a height where neither foot touches the ground in walking, or the lower half will tend to swing.

The walking movement on the stage itself is most easily worked from the performer's right to left. On the return direction it is best to transfer the control bar to the left hand, and work the knee bar either with the point of the index finger in the thumb hole, or with the free right hand.

Costume

The marionettes in the opposite picture belong to the eighteenth century Venetian theatre in the Victoria and Albert Museum. Their clothing provides an example but also a warning.

The silhouette and tone contrast in the costume of each figure is excellent and in this respect they make a good visual effect. However, much of the detail must be lost at a distance, and although these marionettes had a very simple mechanism, the hats at least would get in the way of modern stringing.

There are different opinions on how nearly clothing for puppets should be related to conventional dressmaking.

With loose removable clothing, I feel that proper cutting and sewing are suitable. This sort of clothing can be fastened by hooks and eyes, or press studs, over glove puppets, rod puppets and marionettes. With marionettes, removal for cleaning and pressing is a nuisance as half the strings have to be untied, but I think it is well worth while to be able to give a fresh appearance to a puppet which is used often. With this sort of dressmaking, as with lighting and stage carpentry, some special skill has to be called upon, and there is always at least one girl in the company who can carry out the designs suggested.

Close-fitting clothes are better not to be made by techniques of orthodox dressmaking. Free movements at joints, and particularly at the shoulder joint tend to become restricted. In this case it is better to tack and glue material to give the needed effect, and certain parts can even be included in carving, and be painted. With any type of clothing it is a general rule never to restrict movement at joints, or to push stringing out of line.

In designing clothes for a play, colour and period must be decided upon first. Line and profile are more important than detail, as the visual effect must reach the back row of the audience.

Eighteenth-century Venetian marionettes

Choice of material will depend on the type of puppet to be clothed. With glove puppets I like to have a basic glove of blanket material to give the body substance. Clothes over this may be as thin as you like, and removable for pressing or cleaning.

With marionettes and rod puppets, thick material can give substance where the puppet is made only of jointed dowelling. Where the body is fully carved or padded, thinner material may be used.

In choosing texture, thickness and pattern for puppets' clothes, great care must be taken to relate the material to a very much reduced scale. Hardly any material woven and patterned for the use of full-sized human beings, hangs or drapes easily on a puppet, but where the draping is close to the body, cloth may be damped with size solution and sculptured into folds while wet. This was done with the clothes of the shepherd and shepherdess marionettes shown earlier in this book.

Special effects

The ability of the television camera to isolate the details of a puppet for its audience has developed the taste for extra articulation of facial features. The rod puppet is most suitable for this purpose, and for the extra mechanism of a nodding head, moving eyes or lips it is best to work with a strong hollow laminated *papier maché* head.

A   The nodding movement of the head is on its own a fairly straightforward mechanism. The space where the supporting rod enters the head is enlarged, and a narrow passage is drilled horizontally through the supporting rod. A wire shaft is passed through the *papier maché* head from below one ear, through the passage drilled in the supporting rod and out below the opposite ear. The ends of the wire are turned over with round-nosed pliers and concealed under a further layer of *papier maché*. The head with its wire shaft should now move easily backwards and forwards on its supporting rod.

Two small wire loops are now attached with plastic wood and glued to the front and back edges of the space where the supporting rod enters the head. A small spring or piece of elastic passes from the back loop to a screw-eye fixed in the back of the supporting rod. This holds the head in an upright position. From the front wire loop a length of twine passes through a screw-eye fixed to the front of the supporting rod and down the front of the rod to a trigger attachment at its base. This trigger mechanism is a wire loop passed through a hole drilled in the rod. An extension of the loop can be worked by the thumb alone of the hand holding the rod. Pressure on the trigger lowers the head and on release the pull of the spring above raises the head back to normal position. The joint of head and neck can be concealed by a high collar in the clothing.

B   The articulation of facial features involves more detailed work. Again a hollow *papier maché* head is used, but in this case the modelling is continued downwards to include the hollow shaft of the neck. The supporting rod may be attached to the inside back of the neck, leaving the space inside the head free.

1 The top of the *papier maché* head is cut off with a sharp knife to allow free entry for work inside. This is easily replaced later and the join concealed by the hair.
2 The circles of each eye-ball and upper lid together are cut out, and also the lower lip with a half circle scoop below it.

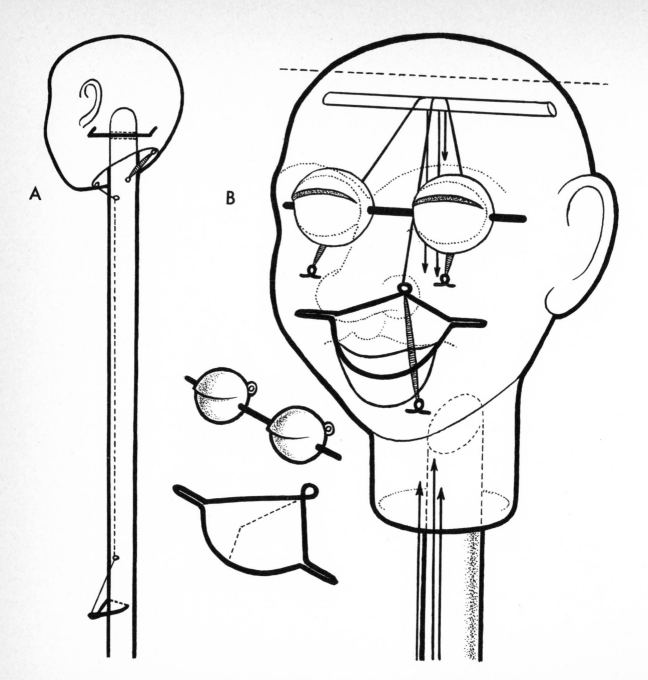

3 The cut out eyes with their upper lids are built from behind into spheres with plastic wood, and a wire loop embedded in each at the back. A wire shaft passes through each eye and its ends are placed in small pellets of plastic wood glued to the inside of the head. As the plastic wood dries the shaft is rotated slightly to form a loose-fitting housing, but the eyes on the shaft must stay fixed.

4 A wire frame, bent into shape with round-nosed pliers as shown in the diagram, is glued to the rim of the lower lip which is strengthened with a coat of plastic wood. The two front pivots of the frame are embedded in plastic wood sockets in the same manner as the shaft for the eyes.

5 A small spring or piece of elastic passes from the loop at the back of the lip frame to the base of the head, keeping the mouth in a closed position. In the same way the loop in the back of each eye is attached to a wire loop behind each cheek and the eyes are held in an open position.

6 Lengths of twine from the wire loops behind the eyes, and from the loop at the back of the lip frame pass over a horizontal length of dowelling fixed in the top of the head, and thence down the front of the supporting rod to trigger mechanisms at its base. Pressure on the triggers closes the eyes and opens the mouth.

An eighteenth-century Venetian marionette theatre

Puppet theatres

The construction of a puppet theatre is a skilled job, and will have to be carried out under the direction of a trained carpenter. For this reason, the drawings and measurements I have given in this section are suggestions only. The theatre you design for yourself must be modified to your own needs, and the following points should be remembered in planning:

Is the theatre to be portable or permanent?
What type and size of puppets are to be used?
Is the theatre to be adaptable for different types of puppet?
How many people are likely to be employed in your productions?

There are two main types of theatre; those for puppets worked from below and those for puppets worked from above. Sometimes one theatre may be used for both by means of a few simple alterations. Most theatres are made of wood framing covered with curtaining or thin hardboard, but the aluminium tubing and stretched canvas of modern camping equipment would be excellent for portable theatres if construction were possible.

The proscenium

The proscenium of the theatre is the screen standing between the audience and the puppet operators. This screen conceals from the audience such mechanics of staging as the producer does not wish to be seen. The drawing on the left shows the proscenium of an eighteenth-century Venetian marionette theatre now belonging to the Victoria and Albert Museum.

Before a performance, and during the intervals, the proscenium is all that the audience have to look at, so it deserves some consideration in design. Unfortunately many portable theatres have nothing more to offer than an expanse of dark curtaining, but a decorative frame round the proscenium opening could certainly be included in the portable equipment. Scenery can also be used before the stage as well as on and behind it.

The proscenium opening

The proscenium opening is the area through which the audience sees the stage and is closed by a curtain before, during the intervals and after the performance.

The position of this opening is important as it must be visible to the whole audience. Usually the lower rim of the opening (stage level) is at least 4 ft high, the average head level of a seated audience. This is no problem in the case of a permanent theatre, but in a portable marionette theatre the bulk of units to be carried can become a problem. Luckily, most halls or lecture theatres already have a stage or rostrum which helps to raise the height, but it is best to have a rostrum of one's own available if necessary. In theatres for puppets worked from below, the height of the proscenium opening is not likely to be a problem; the stage level is usually at the height of the operator's head, which is high enough for everyone to see.

After making sure that your audience can see, make sure that they cannot see too much. Particular care should be taken with the front row. The sight lines from the side chairs may lead beyond the edge of the backcloth and wings, and the centre chairs may have a view over the top of the backcloth to the operators at work. These faults can be dealt with either by altering the curtaining, or moving the position of the chairs.

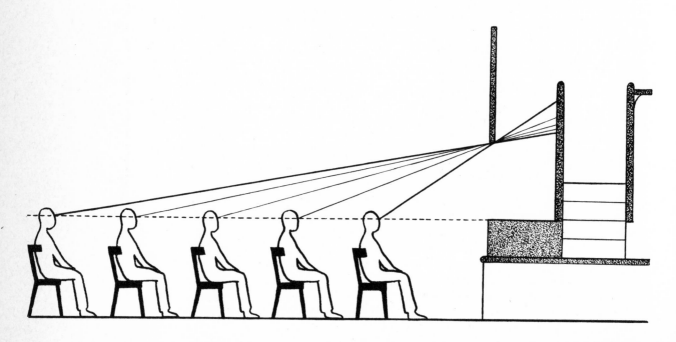

Sight lines to the proscenium opening

A theatre worked from below

Traditionally, glove puppets are manipulated on the upstretched arm, and the lower border of the proscenium opening is level with the operator's head. A good stage level height for adult performers is $5\frac{1}{2}$ ft, but for children the proscenium opening must be lower. The width of the opening depends on the number of performers likely to be employed. The theatre shown here is a simple folding booth for two performers only. It is suitable for glove puppets, rod puppets and, with the addition of a screen, shadow puppets.

The height of the framing is $7\frac{1}{2}$ ft. The wings are $2\frac{1}{4}$ ft wide, and the front panel $4\frac{1}{2}$ ft, so that when closed the wings meet exactly for easy transportation.

The proscenium opening is $5\frac{1}{2}$ ft above floor level, 4 ft wide and $1\frac{3}{4}$ ft high. This is high enough for any glove puppet, but if you are using large rod puppets you may wish to raise the upper border of the opening.

The detachable frame round the proscenium opening has a small projecting ledge on the lower border which serves as a stage floor for such properties as the play demands. The curtain rail and light bar fit behind the top border of the frame.

There are hooks on the inside of the wings on which to hang puppets and an extra shelf may be added for props not in use. The booth may be covered with thin hardboard, although this tends to be heavy, or with hanging curtaining. Pegs along the top of the side wings make divisions for scenery battens.

The whole framework may be made of 3 in. × 1 in. softwood, with 5 in. × 1 in. top and bottom crosspieces for extra strength. Wing nuts and screws join all the separate parts, and are carried separately when the booth is dismantled.

You may find holding glove puppets on the upstretched arm very tiring. Some people prefer to work with the elbow at waist level. A curtain of thin material hangs from a scenery batten between the puppet and the manipulator's head and shoulders, screening them from the audience. As the performer looks through from the dark side of the curtain into the lighted area, he can see without being seen. The depth of movement is limited, but the performer has a better view for checking the action of the play, and a bar slung between the wings of the booth serves as an elbow rest.

For this type of manipulation either a lower proscenium opening must be designed, or a 1-ft high platform is placed within the booth raising the performer to the level of the usual opening.

Both glove and rod puppets may be worked from a seated position or even from movable stools on wheels.

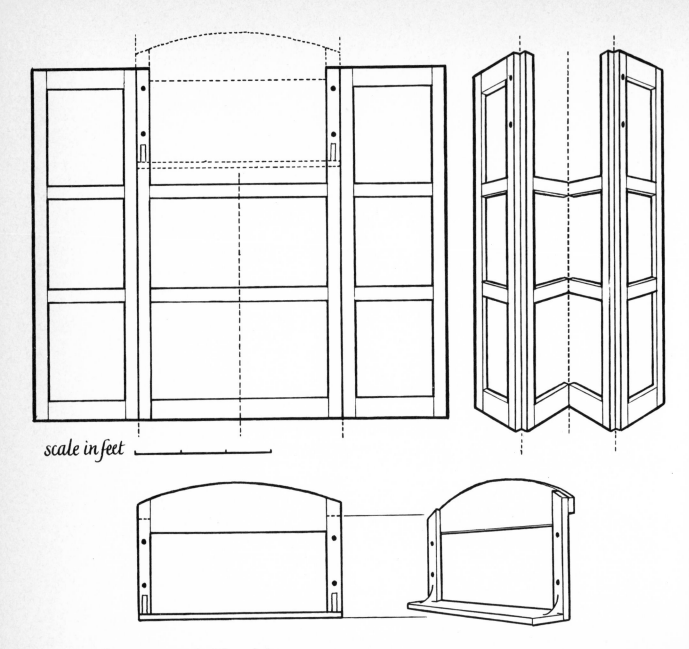

scale in feet

A theatre for puppets worked from below

A theatre for puppets worked from below (partly assembled)

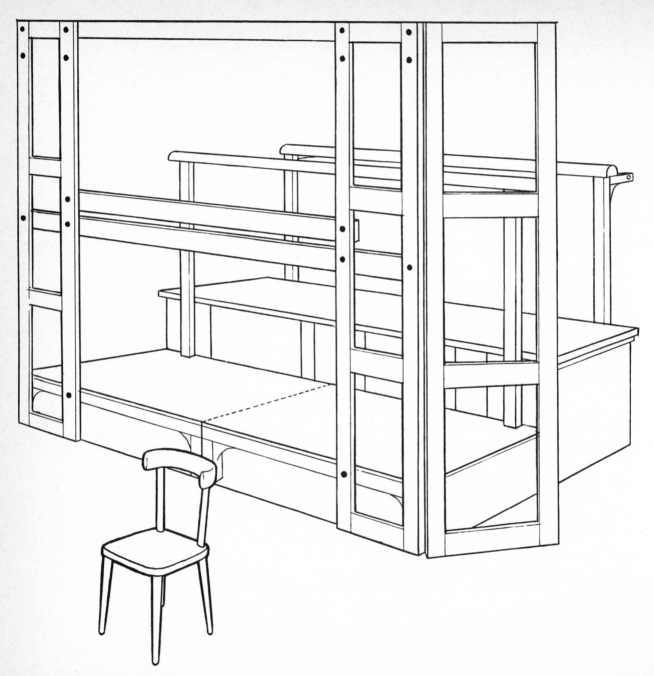

Assembled portable marionette theatre from the front

A portable theatre worked from above

A theatre for marionettes is a good deal more complicated than the puppet booth which has just been described. These are the principle parts which should be found in any marionette theatre.

A *proscenium*, high enough to conceal the manipulators, and a proscenium opening of sufficient height for the audience to be able to see the performance on the stage.

A *stage floor*, level with the lower border of the proscenium opening, for the marionettes to act upon.

A *bridge* behind the stage on which the manipulators stand. The stage back-cloth is hung against this bridge.

A *leaning bar* at the stage side of the bridge, on which the manipulators may rest their elbows.

A *perch bar* at the back of the bridge from which marionettes are hung.

A *curtain rail* above the stage side of the proscenium opening and a light bar above it.

All these parts can be seen in the following drawings.

Most portable marionette theatres I have seen owe a debt to the one designed in America by Gayle Michael Anderson. For those who wish to see a specific plan of this theatre, exact details can be found in *The Puppet Theatre Handbook* by Marjorie Batchelder. The Anderson theatre folds into flat sections of not more than 4 ft 4 in. square.

In the theatre shown here, I have preferred to give a simple outline rather than a detailed account, as most people like to make adjustments to suit their own situation. This theatre was built to be strong and easily assembled and it travelled with a cast of fifteen in a small hired lorry. Some of the sections are 9 ft long, but those who wish for smaller sectioning may break it down further without much difficulty.

The stage of this theatre was designed to be just under $1\frac{1}{2}$ ft high, as it was presumed that there would be a stage or rostrum available in each of the public halls where performances were to be given.

This same theatre may be altered for use with puppets worked from below by moving the light and curtain bars to the top of the proscenium, and moving down the top crossbar to the former position of the light bar.

The proscenium is formed from two folding screens and three crosspieces, two of which are the curtain bar and light bar respectively. The opening in this proscenium is 6 ft wide by 3 ft high.

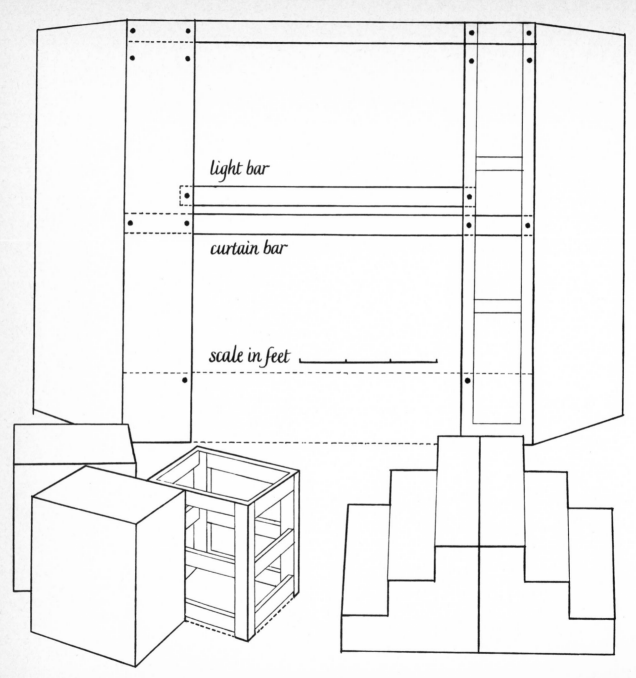

light bar

curtain bar

scale in feet

Parts of portable marionette theatre

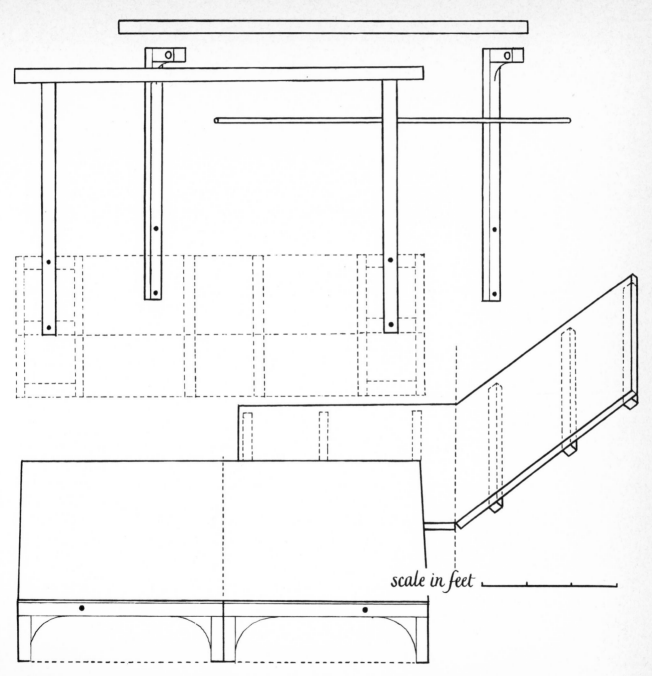

scale in feet

Parts of portable marionette theatre

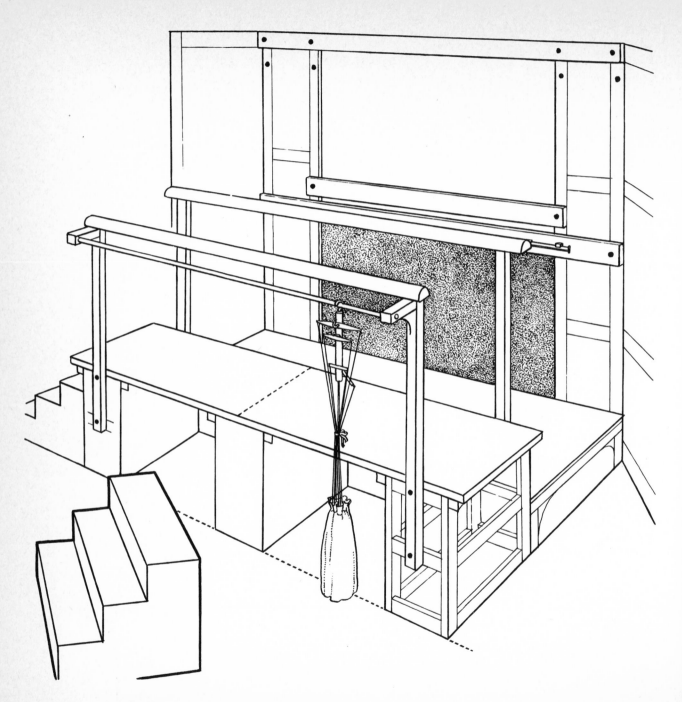

Assembled portable marionette theatre from behind

The stage floor folds in the centre and is bolted in front to the two standing screens.

The operator's bridge is formed from three boxes on which rests the bridge floor. The floor folds in the centre and is made of strong planking. Cross battens fit closely to the sides of the boxes.

The leaning bar is made from two upright posts and one horizontal rail. The uprights are bolted to the framing of the bridge boxes, and overlap the stage to keep it stable.

The perch bar is also made from two upright posts bolted to the outer bridge boxes, and a horizontal rail for safety. The rail from which the marionettes are hung stands clear of the rail at the back of the bridge. It may be made from hardwood dowelling, but a brass rod or even strong cord can be used.

Two step units lie on each side of the operator's bridge.

The whole theatre is fitted together with wing nuts and screws, and the framing is mostly of 3 ft 1 in. softwood. It was found safer to fit a detachable metal bar on either side of the stage from the leaning rail uprights to the proscenium folding screens. Curtains hanging from hooks on the proscenium screen cover the framing during performances.

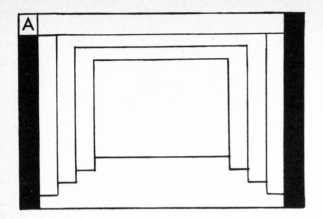

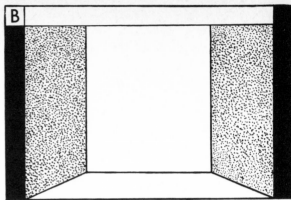

Scenery

Scenery and properties for puppet productions must naturally be in scale with the puppets performing. Properties can be made of the same materials as the puppets themselves—cardboard, *papier maché* and wood. Scenery can be made of thick cardboard with wood framing where necessary, and backcloths from old sheets. Large amounts of paint may have to be used in painting scenery, and I have found that powder paint is the cheapest. Powder paint is mixed with water, and with the addition of a small amount of diluted size crystals, the paint stays fixed on cloth and does not rub off. Before painting a sheet backcloth, a coat of diluted size prepares the surface for painting.

The layout of scenery on the puppet stage must be very simple as all possible space is needed for the performers. The diagrams above show the two basic settings of theatre scenery and each has some application in puppetry.

A   The wing setting is most conveniently used in the theatre for puppets worked from below. These wings may be cut into profiles, or left quite plain and they hang from a wooden rod which rests on the side walls of the booth. An example of this can be seen in the illustration of a partly assembled glove puppet theatre. Puppets are placed from below behind the wings, and then appear as if entering from the side.

In a theatre for marionettes a wing setting interferes with the strings of the puppets and it is safer to depend mainly on a wide backcloth which extends well beyond the limits of the proscenium opening. Backcloths may be kept on a wooden rod, and hung when in use on hooks fixed to the supports of the leaning rail. An example of this can be seen in the frontispiece illustration.

B   The box setting can only be used in the marionette theatre if side rostrums are available, and when entrance doorways are cut right to the top to allow the passage of the marionette strings. A type of box setting can be seen in the drawing of the Venetian marionette theatre. The side walls of the box stop short of the backcloth leaving entrances on either side at the rear of the stage.

With either type of setting the stage floor of the marionette theatre should be covered with a floor cloth to hide carpentry joints, and to deaden the sound of the puppets' movements.

Lighting

To provide safe and effective lighting for a puppet theatre skilled advice is essential. I have included the addresses of stage lighting suppliers at the end of this book. Some of your equipment may be ordered from their catalogues and some may be made for you locally by a professional electrician. What is really important is that you should know what you aim to achieve by your lighting; the simplest and most direct method of carrying it out will be the best.

In deciding on your aims it may be helpful to remember that the first object of lighting is to enable the audience to see on the stage what is important for them to see at the time, and secondly that by changes in strength, contrast and colour, the mood and development of a production can be enhanced.

The particular problems of the puppet theatre lie in the shallowness of the stage which can give an effect of flatness, and the tendency of shadow from rods, strings and puppets to be thrown on the backcloth. I give below a list of equipment which I have found sufficient for most productions.

1 A hanging batten of light bulbs placed in reflectors immediately above the curtain rail behind the proscenium opening

This can be made locally, and if 100-watt bulbs are used in reflector compartments of 8 in. long you can have a row of nine to ten bulbs above a 6-ft stage. In some theatres these bulbs are in groups of red, blue and green with a separate control and dimmer for each group. In theory the three colours used together make a white light although it never has the strength of a row of white bulbs. Also dimmers are expensive and it is cheaper to alter colour by using gelatine slides fitted into grooves in front of each bulb. These slides can be changed between scenes.

2 Lamps either hanging or placed on stands at either side of the stage

These lamps can be floodlamps to give a wide area of light or spotlamps to give a concentrated beam. Where there is little room on a puppet stage one of each will be quite sufficient. Coloured slides can be fitted in front of the flood-lamp when needed. These lamps help to counteract the flat effect of lighting from the front only, and can be directed on to the backcloth to eliminate shadow.

3 Switchboard and dimmers

A 'suitcase' switchboard with dimmers is made by some stage lighting companies and it is very useful for travelling productions. A switchboard has a separate control for each piece of lighting equipment, and ideally a separate dimmer for each circuit. The whole switchboard is fed from a main plug. Each dimmer has the appearance of a lever in a groove, and by raising or lowering the lever the lighting controlled by that circuit is increased or decreased in strength.

As you can see lighting rapidly becomes a complicated and expensive problem. Where the trouble and expense seem unjustified it is perhaps enough to concentrate on the first aim of lighting which is that the performance should be seen.

Permanent marionette theatres

If you are fortunate enough to be establishing a permanent theatre, you will have much more scope for imagination than in the case of a portable one. For obvious reasons portable theatres must be kept simple, and the acting area is seldom more than $2\frac{1}{2}$ ft deep, about as far as any manipulator can reach his control bar over the leaning rail. In a permanent theatre there are various ways of making a deeper and more interesting stage.

Side rostrums can be constructed at the back of the usual $2\frac{1}{2}$-ft stage with an extra depth of acting area between them. This inner stage can be part of the whole scene, or may be concealed by scenery until is is needed.

A centre rostrum at the back of the $2\frac{1}{2}$-ft stage allows the acting area to continue back on either side. The centre rostrum is less easy to incorporate in stage scenery.

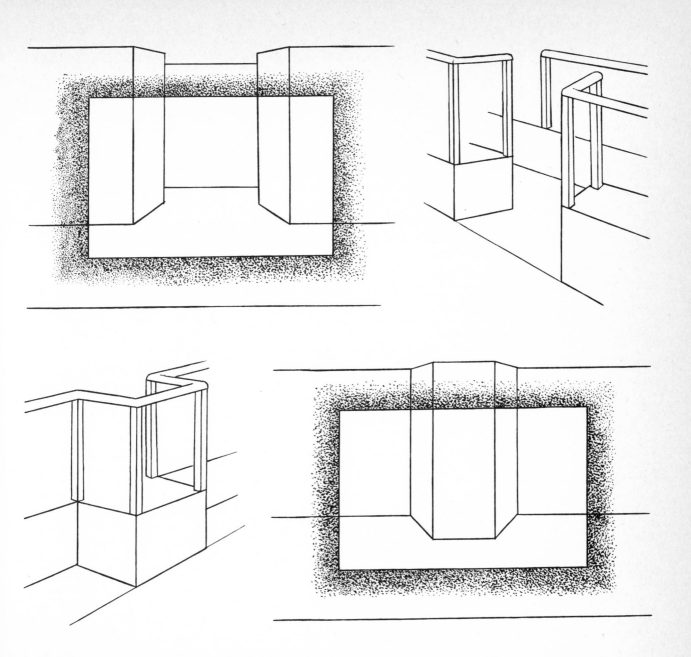

Side rostrums and centre rostrum on a permanent stage

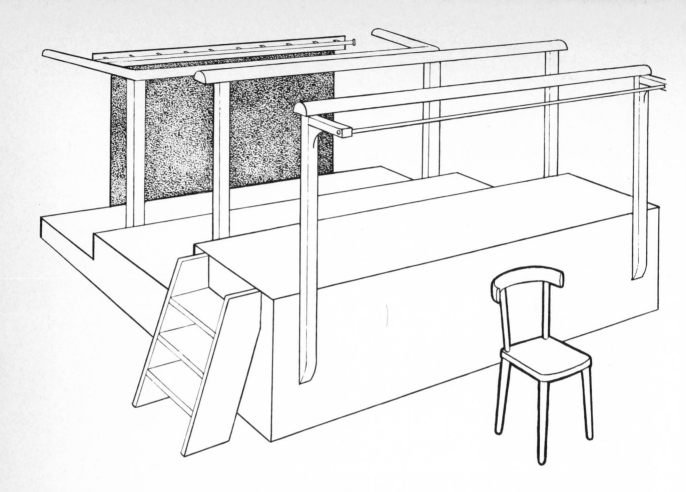

A permanent double-tier stage

You may have a higher second stage behind the first. This second stage can act as a manipulator's bridge when the first is in use, and may have a backcloth of its own ready for a quick change when the performance moves back on to it.

In America sometimes a high extra bridge crosses the stage immediately behind the proscenium. This increases the acting area, as marionettes can be passed from the front to the back bridge.

The Italian marionette theatre often makes use of a high centre bridge across the stage. Marionettes can be worked from either side of it.

All these additions to the ordinary stage give a chance for much more interesting floor patterns, where puppets can walk towards and away from the audience, as well as from one side of the stage to the other.

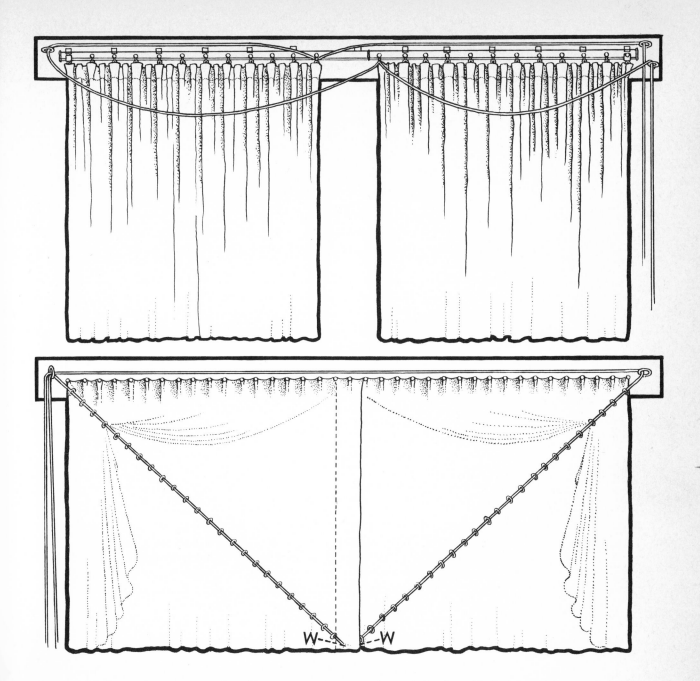

Draw curtains and drape curtains (Drape curtains must be weighted at the inside lower corners)

Production

So much work and ingenuity goes into the making of puppets, that there is sometimes a tendency to neglect the art of production for the skill of the craftsman. From the point of view of an eventual audience, production is of major importance, and planning for the complete performance should begin before the construction of the puppets. Early decisions in production must not only be the choice of play or items for performance, but the size and type of puppet to be used, materials for construction, and plans of colour and period for clothing and scenery. Unless these points are established early there is no chance of unity of style.

Any group of people working together must have a leader in their enterprise and however democratically he may be elected, he must be present to co-ordinate the parts of the whole. Naturally, different responsibilities will be handed to various people, lighting, scenery and costume for instance, but each is aware of the aim of combined work. The director Gordon Craig wrote of his preference for the puppet to the obstructive individuality of the live actor. But even puppets need manipulators, and in amateur shows particularly, personalities and temperament can cause difficulties. Presumably in professional productions the manipulators are more objective and each is paid to perform a defined role. In the end there must be a certain compromise between the personal interpretation of the director, and the individual suggestions of the performers. After all, from the moment it is successfully completed, a puppet develops a life of its own closely linked with its maker or manipulator.

When the puppets have been made, much of the effectiveness of a production rests on a stimulation of the audience by means of various types of contrast, visual and dramatic, in addition to the director's interpretation of the script. The following are some suggestions for visual contrast.

Grouping This is concerned with the visual relationship between puppets at periods of stillness on the stage. This relationship depends mainly on a sense of line and silhouette. The position of an arm or the fall of drapery can help in leading the eye from one puppet to another. In grouping there are contrasts between seated and standing figures, and straight and curved lines.

Floor pattern This is the plan of the position of puppets on a stage as seen from above, both when at rest or in movement. One puppet should never remain immediately behind another where the audience cannot see him, but a variety in the distance of the puppets from the front of the stage gives depth to the scene.

Changes in floor pattern should be well defined. The direction of floor pattern can also lead the audience's attention to the centre of importance on the stage.

Tone value This is the intensity of darks and lights on the stage regardless of colour. Extra focus is given to a puppet dressed in pale colours against a dark background, or alternatively dark against pale. As a general rule I prefer that tone contrasts in a backcloth should be less strong than the tone contrasts in the clothing and complexion of the puppets themselves. This is true to nature where distance is muted, and near objects more sharply defined.

Colour There are two types of colour on the stage—atmospheric colour and local colour. Atmospheric colour has very little to do with contrasts, as it is the general colour shed on the whole stage by the lighting. It may of course be altered in intensity by dimming, or in tint by the use of gelatine slides in the floods at the side of the stage. Local colour is the colour belonging to the actual objects on the stage themselves. Here strong contrasts of warm and cool colours are stimulating.

Dramatic contrasts are likely to arise only in longer narrative productions.

Mood This is concerned with the emotional content of drama, and depends to some extent on the script. If you are successful in creating mood in the emotional response of the audience, it is best not to continue too long without change. At its highest level this can be seen in Shakespearean tragedy where periods of comedy lessen the tension.

Climax A gradual increase of pace and interest to a climax is more likely to hold the attention of your audience than an unvaried progression. A Nativity play has a natural climax when all the separate characters eventually meet in the stable scene at Bethlehem. The climax is no less effective for being expected.

Pause An unvaried speed of conversation and action is dull. A pause gives time for the audience to digest what has happened and to prepare for more. Be careful however. Too often in amateur productions the general pace is already too slow, and a pause only makes things worse.

Having spoken of contrasts, it should also be remembered that a certain unity or continuity is essential in good dramatic production. Classical Greek dramatists observed rules of continuity in time, place, and action. Spectacular and violent events did not take place on stage, but were merely described there. Now there is no reason why contemporary drama should necessarily follow these principles, but they are helpful in forming standards. Also in their reduction of technical difficulties they might have been formed specifically for puppets, particularly marionettes. One can avoid constant scene changing, and unconvincing attempts to reproduce violent action, with a clear conscience.

Standards of taste

For some people the most important object in making puppets is to be as life-like as possible, and there are always those who will only be impressed by winking eyes, moving lips and individual finger movements. These things have their place, most acceptably in television perhaps where the camera can isolate detail in close up, or in cabaret where no staging or illusion hides technique. But there are other standards than these; in the end puppets must behave like puppets.

They are not people, but interpretations of them made in wood, *papier maché* or cloth and wire, and the way in which they move and look results from the material from which they are made. The art of the puppet-maker lies in interpreting the human form in terms of his chosen material, and this involves limitation and discipline. The history of any craft shows that its standards were highest when the nature of the medium used was most fully understood while its limitations were recognised and accepted. These standards always degenerate when material is abused in the attempt to reach a scope not natural to it.

There is a tendency today to use many materials or multimedia in art forms. Although this makes many things possible which would not be possible with only one medium, the removal of discipline and limitation usually results in a lack of style. The end product is characteristic of nothing in particular.

In working with puppets one must always be aware of a sense of scale. Puppets are usually fairly small beings. It is surprising how often in professional productions the movements of 2-ft high marionettes are accompanied by the recorded background music of a full symphony orchestra! Puppetry is an intimate art, more successful in the home than in a theatre, and care should be taken not to swamp a performance with accessories unrelated in scale. Live music has much more impact than recorded music with puppets, and a single piano, recorders, guitar or children's voices singing make a happier combination.

What then is the real nature of puppets? I think, with the exception of the glove puppet which moves with the human hand, that their limitations make them best suited to a stylised form of movement as in mime or dancing. Reality is for them to interpret or suggest, not to imitate.

Rehearsing

Rehearsals are most successful when they progress in stages. This allows for adjustment and experiment, and exchange of ideas between the director who sees the production as a whole, and the manipulators who will have their own ideas about the puppets which they have made.

1   Before meeting together on the stage, each manipulator must practise on his own with his puppet to understand its movements. This is best done in front of a mirror to see the audience's view, and with a marionette the operator can stand on a chair and prop a mirror on the floor in front of him. Although from the beginning each puppet has been constructed to perform certain actions, free play helps to develop the character of the puppet in the performer's mind, and new effective movements may be discovered by accident. With practice the manipulator's thinking and feeling becomes transferred immediately to the puppet's movement.

2   First rehearsals on the stage are drawn from separate groups of performers. This may be done by practising one scene at a time, only those concerned in each scene being present. There is no need at this stage to combine speech and action. In these rehearsals the director can establish floor pattern and movement and arrange grouping for moments of rest. Difficulties of manipulation such as the passing of one performer behind another at the leaning bar can be practised or eliminated. If it is essential that one puppet be passed in front of another during the action, either the manipulators can exchange puppets or one manipulator can hold both while the other passes behind him on the bridge.

Other separate groups who may rehearse on their own are scene changers, musicians, property managers, lighting technicians and speakers if the speaking parts are performed separately from the manipulation.

3   Once movement and grouping have been established speaking and movement must be co-ordinated. It is very important here that the puppets should look at one another when speaking, that movement and speech are synchronised and that other puppets remain quite still so that the attention of the audience is not distracted. There may still be a certain amount of further suggestion and alteration in staging as the dramatic sequence becomes more familiar.

4   Later rehearsals become for the performers largely a matter of remembering and repeating actions and words which should now be established and unchanged. If music be included in a production it should be part of rehearsals from now on, so that the director can see the pace of the complete performance. It will almost certainly be necessary for him to increase the speed of certain sections, and to point out contrasts where they can be effective.

5   Lighting can be added last and is a final stimulant to the performers. By allowing rehearsals to progress in this way a performance grows as if alive, and does not become a stale repetition. The addition of new elements right up to the end of rehearsals keeps up the interest of the performers and guards against the danger of over-rehearsal.

Sources of suitable material for performance

It would be easy enough at this stage to say, 'Go to your local library and see what plays written for puppets they have to offer.' You can do this, and decide for yourself just what you think of the material available. Unfortunately, in the English and American puppet theatre, plays have been handed down by word of mouth and seldom in written form. Such writing for puppet performance that you will find will be mainly contemporary, and major writers are very seldom represented. Of the material used in the seventeenth and eighteenth centuries, the finest period in the history of the English puppet, there is hardly a trace. This means that you must improvise and adapt for yourself from fantasy, burlesque, biblical stories, folk legend, historical drama and any contemporary work that may be presented in terms of the puppet.

For those who are determined to find plays specifically written for marionettes, some research may bring to light translations of French and Japanese puppet plays.

Effective adaptations can be made from Jacobean drama which has a bravura nature very suitable to glove puppets. There is an added historical interest here for the audience as these plays are seldom performed. The legends and dramas of ancient Greece are also very suitable for puppet performance. The original presentation of Greek drama had a discipline not unlike that of the marionette. Principal actors spoke through masks and movements were highly stylised.

Children will always find a great fund of material in the fantasy of folklore and fairy tales, and are always very happy to improvise. It is not necessary however to have a narrative script for every type of performance. I give below a list of different types of production in order of complexity.

Movement only with music or sound effects

This may be effectively presented in variety acts or dance movements, but only if the manipulation is perfect and the techniques elaborate enough to be interesting. Without these qualifications it is unlikely that the attention of an audience can be held.

Movement with spoken commentary

This is my own favourite type of performance and it is particularly suited to shadow puppets and to marionettes. The movement of the puppets is a mimed interpretation of the story which is narrated by one person at the same time. The whole production is simple, it may be accompanied by music, and there is none of the trouble of synchronising movement with actual speech. Folk ballads and narrative poetry of all countries and ages may be used.

Movement with words spoken by the manipulators

For this type of performance a specially written play or transcription with parts is necessary. The direct relation between speech and movement is most easily carried out by glove or rod puppets. Either type of puppet may have the addition of lip movement. Plays involving well-defined personalities and rapid action are particularly suitable here and the story of Punch and Judy is an excellent model. Always remember the ability of the glove puppet to hold, to lift and to throw.

Movement with parts spoken separately from manipulation

Quite complicated performances can be carried out by this method, and if marionettes are to be used with spoken parts this is the best arrangement. Problems of space behind stage must be considered as the speakers should be able to see the puppets. Some people tape-record the speaking parts beforehand. I have never liked this method as the puppets must then be moved in time with the recorded sound, which makes no allowance for accidental delays in movement.

Audience participation in a performance

This can be done with live performers 'planted' in the audience. I have done this with the Artisans Play from *A Midsummer's Night's Dream*. The parts of the artisans were taken by glove puppets and Theseus and Hippolyta sat among the audience who were very surprised when they joined in the conversation. In a variety act audience participation may be unrehearsed.

The illustrations used in this book are from Hans Andersen (shadow puppets), the Artisans Play from '*A Midsummer Night's Dream*' (glove puppets), '*The Emperor and The Little Girl*' by Bernard Shaw (marionettes) and a Nativity Play by Laurence Houseman (marionettes).

Suppliers of materials

Arts and crafts shops

CARDBOARD for children's theatre and shadow puppets; PAPER all thicknesses for plans, tracing and shadow scenery; PASTE, GLUE and INDIAN INK for painting shadow puppets; CRAFT or MAT KNIVES and MODELLING CLAY for *papier maché*; PLASTICINE for modelling heads and to aid in casting; WATERCOLOUR PAINT for children's theatre; POWDER PAINT for scenery; OIL PAINT and POSTER PAINT both for painting wooden and *papier maché* puppets; MACRAMÉ TWINE or NYLON FISHING LINE for string joints; PICTURE FRAMER'S PINS for leather joints; SUGAR PAPER for laminated *papier maché*; PAINT BRUSHES and SPIRIT VARNISH for preparing *papier maché* for painting; LEATHER for leather joints.

Painters and decorators shops

CEILING WHITING POWDER for *papier maché*; GLUE and SIZE CRYSTALS for *papier maché* and to mix with powder paint for scenery.

Hardware shops

WIRE all thicknesses for shadow puppet rods, framework for *papier maché* marionettes, brackets for toy theatre actors and for tongue and groove joints; BROOM HANDLES for construction of marionette control bars.

Chemists' shops (Drug stores)

PAPER HANDKERCHIEFS and PAPER TOWELLING for *papier maché*; PLASTER OF PARIS for plaster casts; VASELINE for lining plaster moulds; ROLLER BANDAGING or ADHESIVE TAPE for building cores for direct *papier maché* modelling.

Carpenters' tool shops

All CARPENTERS' TOOLS for making wooden puppets; TABLE VICE, ELECTRIC SANDER and SMALL SCREW EYES for marionettes; WING NUTS and BOLTS for portable theatres; NAILS, SCREWS and WASHERS for marionette control bars.

Sports shops

FISHING TWINE for marionette stringing.

Model kit shops

WOODEN DOWELLING all thicknesses for marionette control bars, puppets' limbs and centre rods of rod puppets; PLYWOOD and PLASTIC WOOD for lining moulds and for fitting inside puppet heads for special mechanisms. WOOD GLUES.

Timber merchant (Lumber yard)

SOFT WOOD for marionette body and limbs; LIME or FRUIT WOOD for puppet head and hands.

Woolworths

CUP HOOKS for marionette control bars, neck joints and waist joints; SIMPLE ELECTRIC FITTINGS; CURTAIN FITTINGS; rails, hooks and fixtures for theatre draw curtains.

Useful waste materials

REMNANTS OF CLOTH, FUR and LAMBSWOOL for puppets' clothes and hair; UMBRELLA RIBS for rods for rod puppets; OLD NYLON STOCKINGS for cloth marionettes; CELLULOID and COLOURED CELLOPHANE WRAPPINGS for coloured insets for shadow puppets; USED COTTON SHEETS for shadow screens; USED BLANKET MATERIAL for glove puppet gloves; NEWSPAPER for *papier maché*; USED LEATHER GLOVES for leather hinge joints; USED TENNIS BALLS for glove puppet heads; SPRINGS from USED BALL POINT PENS and CIGARETTE LIGHTERS for mechanism of special movements.

For wholesale ordering of materials in England the catalogues of the following suppliers will be found helpful:

Dryad Handicrafts, Northgate, Leicester
Nottingham Handicrafts, Nottingham
Atlas Handicrafts, Manchester 4

For ordering materials through the mail in America the following suppliers will be helpful:

American Handicrafts Co. Inc, 20 West 14 Street, New York, New York

Arthur Brown and Bros Inc, 2 West 46 Street, New York, New York

Al Friedman, 25 West 45 Street, New York, New York

For stage lighting equipment catalogues can be ordered from:

Strand Electric and Engineering Co. Ltd, 29 King Street, London W C 2

W. J. Furse & Co. Ltd, 9 Carteret Street, London S.W.1

Times Square Lighting, 318 West 47 Street, New York, New York

Bibliography

General

The Puppet Theatre Handbook
Marjorie Batchelder, Harpers, New York 1946
Herbert Jenkins, London

Puppets and Plays: A Creative Approach
Marjorie Batchelder, Harpers, New York 1956

The Puppet Theatre
Jan Bussel, Faber, London 1946

Hand Puppets and String Puppets
Waldo Lanchester, Dryad, Leicester 1948

Practical Puppetry
J. Mulholland, Arco Publications, New York 1962

Puppetry
Desmond MacNamara, Arco Publications, New York 1965

Puppetry Today
Helen Binyon, Studio-Vista London 1966, Watson Guptill
New York 1966

Marionettes

Puppets into Actors
Olive Blackham, Rockcliff, London 1948

The Marionette
George Merten, Thomas Nelson & Sons 1957

Presenting Marionettes
Susan French, Reinhold, New York 1964

History

History of the English Puppet Theatre
George Speaight, Plays, Boston, Harrap & Co London 1955

Juvenile Drama: The History of the English Toy Theatre
George Speaight, MacDonald, London 1947

History of Java (Vol. 1, chapter VII)
Stamford Raffles, John Murray, London 1817

Punch and Judy
Illustrated by George Cruikshank, John P. Collier, Lacy, 4th
edition 1859

Costume

Costume in Antiquity
James Lever, Thames & Hudson, London 1964, Potter, New
York

Costume through the Ages
James Laver, Thames & Hudson, London 1964, Simon and
Schuster 1964 (both are available in paperback editions)

Principles of Puppet Production

The Art of the Puppet Theatre
Bill Baird, The Ridge Press Book and Macmillan, New York
1965

The Marionette
Ed. Gordon Craig, Florence, 1918, Theatre Arts, New York
1925 'The Actor and the Uber-Marionette'
From *On the Art of the Theatre*, Heinemann, London 1911

Folk Plays for Puppets you can Make
Tom H. Tichenor, Abingdon, New York 1959